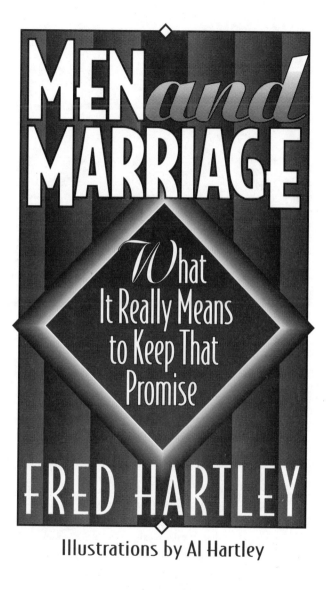

MEN and MARRIAGE

What It Really Means to Keep That Promise

FRED HARTLEY

Illustrations by Al Hartley

BETHANY HOUSE PUBLISHERS
Minneapolis, MN 55438

Published by Bethany House Publishers
A Ministry of Bethany Fellowship, Inc.
11300 Hampshire Avenue South
Minneapolis, Minnesota 55438

Printed in the United States of America

Library of Congress Cataloging-in-Publication Data

Hartley, Fred.
    Men and marriage : what it really means to keep that promise / Fred
Hartley III.
        p.   cm.

    1. Husbands—Religious life.   2. Marriage—Religious aspects—
Christianity.   I. Title.
BV4528.2.H37   1994
248'425—dc20   94–8450
ISBN 1–55661–450–0   CIP

To the two most influential "promise keepers" in my life—
my dad

Al Hartley

who did more for me than he will ever realize
by loving my mom
and
my dad-in-law

Bob Dykstra

who did more for me more than he will ever realize
by setting an example of a godly man
for my wife

FRED HARTLEY III is the author of eight books, including the bestseller *Dare to Be Different* and *The Teenage Book of Manners, Please!* He is a graduate of Wheaton College and Gordon-Conwell Theological Seminary and is presently the Senior Pastor of Lilburn Alliance Church in metro Atlanta. He and his wife of twenty-one exciting years have four children.

CONTENTS

Section I: There Is Hope

Section II: There Is Help

Section III: There Is Dignity

Section One

THERE IS HOPE

Most men walk around with too much weight on their shoulders. Just add it all up—a wife, career, kids, mortgage payments, leaky faucets, taxes, civic clubs, exercise, church work, family budget . . . Yikes! If anyone tries to carry all that responsibility, sooner or later something will snap.

A cartoon in an airline magazine recently caught my attention. It graphically illustrated a problem many men have felt. When I read it, I laughed out loud. In the background looms a large suburban two-story home silhouetted against a night sky. From an upstairs bedroom the teenage daughter yells, "Dad, can I go out with Mike Friday night?" From the teenage boy's room, "Dad, can I have the keys to the car?" The grade school kid screams, "Dad, can you help me with geography?" The grandmother is saying from her sitting room, "Son, did you have my TV antenna fixed?" The baby is crying "Da-da!!" from the nursery, and the wife holding the phone in the kitchen announces, "Honey, it's for you! . . . Honey, are you home?" With all this activity coming from the house in the background, in the foreground we see the husband-father dug into a foxhole, decked out with a pith helmet and fatigues, clutching a sign that reads: "Off Duty!"

After I chuckled, I handed the cartoon to the passenger seated next to me and he too laughed out loud. "Wow! I have felt exactly like that! In fact, I feel like that most of the time." For the rest of our trip from L.A. to Atlanta we compared notes.

"Honey, are you home?" is a question with dubious distinction. It carries with it a sense of belonging, a sense of being needed, and hopefully a sense of affection—all of which are positive. The downside of the question is that it carries with it a heavy weight of responsibility, and at times the weight seems to be more than we can shoulder.

Many good men are asking themselves, "How did I buy into all this?" Initially all they wanted was a wife, kids, and a decent job. Then suddenly they find themselves sprinting from duty to duty, never able to catch their breath.

Before we reach for answers, let's take time to make sure we understand the real questions. At the end of this book are some study guide questions that you may find helpful as you read.

While most marriage books have a feminine twang, with rosebuds and pink covers laced with perfume, the book in your hands is categorically different. Right from the start let's set the record straight. WARNING: This book is written for the sole use of men who are married. Anyone else reading the material may find it hazardous to his or her health. If you are neither male nor married, please close the book immediately and give it to someone who qualifies. Any husband who catches his wife reading this book or using its contents against him is free to blow a whistle, throw a yellow flag, or assess a penalty.

If, however, you are a man who is married, I guarantee that sometime during this first section, you will feel as if you are sitting down with someone who understands your sore spots and your stress points. And, yes, we will discover together, there *is* hope.

"Honey, Are You Home?"

Most men think about running away from home at some time in their lives, but few actually follow through with it. At least, few follow through as dramatically as George did.

George was a reasonably successful businessman in a small Connecticut town. He had invested most of his energy in a bakery and was able to open two satellite stores, which together generated a decent income. Despite a hectic and demanding career, he still found time for his wife, four children, church, and even civic clubs. But when the demands of accumulated responsibility took their toll, he began to see himself as a man on a treadmill. Others respected him, but when the income from his business didn't justify the Herculean effort it took, the hopeless situation drained his spirit more than anyone could have predicted. Without any warning or explanation, one day George packed his bags and walked out. He walked out on his bakery business, his family, his church life, and his community involvement. He wadded up his duties, tossed them into the wastepaper basket, and skipped town. He left no note, notified no friends, and left no clues. For the next few months his wife, family, and friends listed him with the FBI as a "missing person." In one bold stroke, he simply checked out. George's family did not hear a single word from him for seven years. True story.

Not everyone feels as much stress as George did, but many of us have felt the cold shadow of desperation that obviously weighed on his spirit till he chose to flee. Shouldering the weight of a career, a marriage, a family, a home, a budget, along with church and civic duties, is enough to make any healthy man want to dip into his sick leave.

A friend told me recently, "I am too busy. Time off without any responsibilities sounds so good to me right now that I have given serious thought to robbing a bank just so I could get caught and thrown in jail where I would have no responsibilities for the next six months."

As I walked away from him, I shook my head and said to myself, *That's scary.* Not because he said it, but because I have felt exactly the same way. I asked myself, *How could sitting in jail sound better than living a normal life—or at least my normal life?* The more I thought, the more it seemed that the answer might really be quite simple. If my normal life is so stressful, or messed up that sitting in a prison cell seems preferable, then I must have already lost my freedom.

A man can lose his freedoms quite quickly and not even realize it. Not at first anyway. Before we know what's happened, we find our time is so committed we no longer make free choices. Many choices are already being made for us; and all we have to do is show up at the right place at the right time and fulfill our assigned duties. Why is it that when we set out to find our niche in life— to choose our mate, to get our home, to settle into our career— our choices seemed so good to us? Why is it that that same choice can come to feel like limitation, a burden, a trap? Is this what we chose? Why didn't someone older, wiser, warn us that along with the love and joy, we were giving up freedoms? And once we lose our freedoms, we will soon lose heart.

No Respect

Every man has a seed planted deep inside that needs to be nurtured regularly with a sense of dignity. When the respect that dignity requires is not given, something very significant begins to die.

Many men can do a pretty good Rodney Dangerfield imitation; they all have their own version of "I don't get no respect."

When a highly demanding job is coupled with a low level of appreciation, sooner or later the most conscientious, highly qualified people will feel like quitting.

One of the primary sources of dignity is responsibility. Deep down we all thrive on responsibility. Throughout adolescence we cried out for it, perhaps even demanded it. We wanted to decide how to spend our time and money, how to wear our clothes and hair and when to come home. The human spirit thrives on responsibility because with that comes the opportunity for creativity, leadership, development, management, advancement, and success. These are the elements that feed the sense of dignity within us. For men who are married, the home is designed to be the place where the seed of dignity is nurtured. A serious problem develops, however, when the very sources that are intended to feed our inner dignity begin to destroy it.

Though the human spirit thrives on responsibility, it is also crushed under the weight of too many obligations, or duties carried far too long without a break. Whether we care to admit it or not, we all have our limitations. When our freedom to assume responsibility becomes a yoke around our necks, when we no longer make free choices because all our choices seem to have already been made for us, and when we forget the meaning of "free time," our sense of fulfillment begins to fade in a hurry.

No, most of us are not like George: We know it's "not manly" to run from responsibilities. Instead, we learn to run faster to keep up with all our duties. Faster . . . and faster. Like rats on a treadmill, we soon find ourselves running frantically, with no change of scenery. We sprint through life, putting forth an enormous amount of energy just to keep the machinery moving. But then it becomes monotony. And soon our lives seem more like a vicious plot to do us in than a set of choices we made willingly.

Treadmills

I pastor a growing church in fast-paced Atlanta, and while I enjoy my job, there are times when I feel abused. Some days I feel as if too many people push my buttons. On one particular day recently, I felt as though every single button in me had been pushed.

I had counseled with three couples whose marriages were being held together by Scotch tape and shoe strings. I tried to encourage them to face their problems honestly, but the process sapped more energy than I could spare. I had been in the office since 6 A.M. for the third day in a row. That afternoon I learned that my father had prostate cancer and my sister was being served divorce papers. A church leader called to tell me that he and his wife thought I was doing a lousy job as their pastor. When I left my study that afternoon, I felt more than wounded. I felt trampled on . . . and I felt like walking out.

As I drove to pick up my two teenaged children at soccer and baseball practice, I was saying to myself, *I don't need this. I am bone tired. I am overextended and I feel like checking out of life. It's just not worth the effort.*

And I knew that my day was not over. But I honestly did not feel like talking with my children, going home, relating to my wife, and shouldering any of the domestic responsibilities that awaited me.

As it happened, I was driving home with my kids in the car when a billboard sign caught my eye. In fact, it more than caught my eye; it slapped cold water on my face. On a solid black background, the white letters seemed to scream at me:

More Men
Run Away From Home
Than Teenagers

Was that what I really wanted—to abandon everything? I knew the answer right away. *No!* But I was allowing myself to be driven by the machinery; consequently even the most important people in my life seemed like enemies.

And that is sick.

I glanced across the front seat of my Mazda and looked my fifteen-year-old eyeball to eyeball. He was half smiling at me and he asked, "Did you read that sign, Dad?"

I sighed. "Yeah. I sure did, son." We drove on in silence, and I was able to do some sorting—separating out areas where I was trying to give more than I *could* give, more than I *should* give—relieved to know that really my heart hadn't drifted from what was important to me. I had only allowed too many matters of lesser importance, relatively speaking, crowd out the greater loves.

It was amazing how, at that moment, so much excess baggage fell off my shoulders. No, I was not about to pack my bags and leave home. That was never the real issue. But my frustration over too many responsibilities had made me resentful toward some of the people I loved most deeply.

Since that day—when my internal priorities came into focus again—I have felt a new clarity, even about the rough times at work. I'm one of those people who ordinarily enjoys his job. It's challenging and rewarding—yet I hate the effect it has on my heart when it's in overload. I, like every other healthy person, hate to feel used and abused, and unrewarded. I'm convinced that I have dignity, and every area of life is intended to reflect a level of significance. Therefore, I've come to the conclusion that unrewarding treadmills are inappropriate for people. They may be okay for lab rats, but treadmills are no place for husbands.

Are certain aspects of your life like a treadmill? Or is it your whole life?

Treadmills can come in all shapes and sizes. We get on them without knowing it. Without realizing how we got that way, we can find ourselves exhausted, panting for breath, and begging for an excuse to climb off. Here are just a few guys who would love to get off:

- The personnel manager whose job requires him to arrive at the office by 6 A.M., prepare work orders, oversee a staff of twelve, and report to local and district managers . . . all without enough support help, and without a pay raise in two years. . . . Without a promotion in sight. When he parks his Pinto every day next to his boss's Mercedes, he swallows his anger and envy. And when he drives home twelve hours later, he has little energy left for his family. He doesn't even feel good about himself. Unfortunately, when he doesn't feel much better, he disappears into his easy chair in front of the tube.

- The husband who brings home a decent paycheck, keeps his lawn mowed, cars washed, and checkbook balanced, yet feels as though he gets nothing but criticism from his wife. But there is a secretary at the shipping firm where he works who *does* appreciate the good job he does.

- The father who can't find time to spend with his teenaged children—and when he does find time, they seem preoccupied with their sports and parties and life outside the home. He feels himself losing control and wonders whether or not his influence is even needed anymore. He fights a sense of failure every time he and his son argue over politics. Maybe the kid should just leave . . . or maybe the problem is that he as the father has already checked out on his son long ago.

- The genuinely spiritual man who wants to express his commitment to God through a local church, but who can't keep all the plates spinning at one time. He wonders if he should forget this spiritual stuff, build his career, and develop his inner life when he's sixty-five and retired.

- Any man who drags his weary frame out of bed at 5:30 A.M., five days a week, fifty weeks a year . . . so he can take his family on a two-week vacation wherever *they* want him to go. One day he will wake up with a desire to smell a different pot of coffee brewing because inside he's screaming out for a break from the monotony.

All of these case studies share at least one common denominator—they involve duty without dignity. Duty without dignity is deadly.

This book is written to help you rediscover your true dignity—and more than that, to help you learn how important it is to cultivate that seed of dignity. And when we do that, something of great spiritual significance will take place in the relationships we treasure most. When we begin to experience dignity and significance at home, among those God has given into our care, then there is little in this world that can take us down and keep us down for long.

As men, we are more than a meal ticket. We have purpose and meaning, and that truth must begin to resonate in us. And once we believe it, others will begin to catch on.

Going Home

Seven years after George walked out on his family in Connecticut, the FBI located him in California. He had traveled across the country, sleeping on park benches, earning a little money as a cook in two-bit restaurants, with no friends and no responsibilities. Eventually, he wanted to go home and reunite with his family, and made it as far east as Utah. But the enormity of his failure overwhelmed him, and for a long time he couldn't continue. Though his family wanted to retrieve him, he would not allow them to come and find him in this condition. By long-distance phone he promised to return to them on his own.

George arrived back in Connecticut for Christmas. When he stepped off the train, none of his children even recognized him. It had been too long, and he had changed radically. They had changed too, and their expectation of what a father was—what a father could be—was virtually nonexistent.

George's presence meant more to his wife than to anyone else. She preferred to have a husband who was only a shadow than to have no husband at all. Not many wives would wait so patiently, and not many would allow their husbands back into their homes under these conditions. As it happened, George did not live long after his return.

Why did George return home? I believe he was answering the call of a deep instinct—the desire every man has to find dignity and meaning and inner fulfillment among their families. George was trying to find his way back like a homing pigeon.

My heart moves from this true story—of a man who literally ran away—to the hundreds of thousands of other men who deep down *want* to but won't. Not outwardly anyway. Their evacuation is a far more subtle departure of the heart—that thought about another woman with a prolonged glance in her direction, that dream about getting in the car one day and just driving . . . and never looking back.

Sure, this departure may be secret and private. But the truth is, it is *not* harmless, or innocent. The subtle, secret, silent departure is dangerous—a first step on the way to real breaks, real departures. The big, sad, painful kinds. These "invisible" departures account for why only 30% of the men in this country claim to be sexually faithful to their wives.

When a man stops receiving dignity in his home life, something within begins to wander. He may or may not diagnose his wanderlust, but one thing is for sure—it cannot continue for long. Sooner or later he and his family will begin to suffer.

The fact is, some of us need to learn how to *check in* to the lives we've chosen before we *check out*.

What about you? Is it time for you to look more closely at what attracted you to your lifestyle in the first place? When you dig down to the bottom of the pile—down underneath all the excess baggage and hyper-extended responsibilities—chances are you will find a long-lost guy who just wants to feel that he and his life are good for something.

Finding Your Way Again

If you have ever felt like checking out, dropping out, waving the off-duty flag—if you have ever secretly wanted to run away from home, if you are tired of the monotony of the rat race and feel like leaping off the treadmill—if you have a sneaking suspicion that you are missing something significant, then you have made a more valuable discovery than if you'd won a million dollars. You may be on the verge of discovering a God-given desire to find dignity and fulfillment within the life you have already chosen, among the people you love from the bottom of your heart. That is a great starting point for a new beginning.

It is my conviction that there is nothing more fulfilling in the life of a man who is married than learning to be a successful husband and father. The position of husbanding is a high-level executive position that brings with it the highest level of dignity. It carries with it all the challenge, management, leadership, creativity, and development as well as opportunities for advancement and success that any man could ever look for.

To begin, it's time that most of us learned how to change that vital key to every man's inner life—*perspective*. Let me show you what I mean, beginning with the biggest choice you and I ever made—the choice of a life partner. . . .

The Morning After

One thing I've learned about marriage in twenty quick years—it is not for cowards. Actually, it took me less than twenty-four hours to come to that conclusion.

We were all alone in our honeymoon condominium on a small, secluded island off the west coast of Florida. For months now every gland in my body had been secreting hormones that were screaming for fulfillment. I felt like a woman in the delivery room who wanted to push. As far as I was concerned our relationship was ten centimeters dilated and fully effaced; the contractions were three minutes apart and the confines of the single life were more than I could bear.

The details of our first night together will be forever locked up in the treasure chest of my own memories, although I will tell you, it was well worth the wait. Our first night together was wonderful, more than wonderful, better than words can express. But the next morning was a complete shocker.

When I awoke with the morning sun slapping me in the face, I rolled over and looked into the face of my bride. So far, so good. There she was. Her huge brown eyes glistened. She obviously had been waiting silently for me to awaken. We were lying in bed together with absolutely nowhere to go—no deadlines, no agenda, no appointments, and no meter running. At first we didn't say anything; we didn't need to. Our eyes saw more within each other than we had ever seen before; the view was more than our souls could contain. We embraced, we felt secure, we were fully committed to each other, and our affection was safe within the covenant of marriage. We giggled, we stared, and we embraced again. Who knows how long this fascination continued? I assure you that neither of us was keeping time. After what seemed like an epoch of infatuation, Sherry whispered, "I am yours . . . all yours . . . and I love it that way," followed by another long embrace. Then, "Fred, you make a pretty good roommate," and "Let's spend the rest of our lives together," and other playful commentary. I loved it. Without saying a word, I basked in the radiance of my bride's affection.

I gradually began to notice something inside that I had not anticipated; butterflies began swarming from the pit of my stomach. "You're my husband, my one and only," she continued as she gleamed with open-faced confidence and dignity. I began to silently rebuke myself. *Calm down, you fool! You have no exams tomorrow; there are no bill collectors banging at the door. Just enjoy this moment.* No matter how I tried, the same tinges of anxiety would flutter to the surface. *What is happening?* I couldn't figure it out. It was obviously only happening inside me; Sherry was as tranquil in her spirit as the sea breeze drifting in our open window, but there I was becoming a border-line basket case.

As I reached for some clothes I was disappointed in myself for feeling insecure, and I was somewhat confused about the source of my insecurity. When Sherry went to the kitchen to prepare a pot of fresh coffee to go with our cinnamon buns, I sat on the porch, hung my head in my hands, and sighed very innocently, *What have I gotten myself into?*

As I look back on that moment now, I can't help but grin, but at the time it was no laughing matter. *What have I gotten myself into?* I sighed again. It was only a vague sense, one I could hardly name. But it felt like a weight—the weight of being responsible for another human being besides myself for the first time at a far deeper level than I'd ever known. It suddenly felt ominous. No longer would my life be governed according to the principle "Look out for yourself." From now on I would maintain equal responsibility for Sherry; in fact, if it came to a choice, I'd put her first. Yikes! My insecurity was not generated because I married the wrong person, or because I had married her too soon. The problem was simply that I was married. For the first time that thought scared me to death.

Prior to our wedding day, marriage was such a logical choice, but now it reverberated with all sorts of intimidating emotional consequences. There was certainly nothing ill-conceived about Sherry's bedroom expressions of trust, commitment, loyalty, and affection. They were genuine, pure and entirely appropriate, but the effect they registered in my heart was awesome—almost terrifying! The carefree single lifestyle that I had said goodbye to only hours earlier was now forever removed from me. All the restrictions of the single life were now lifted, but the obligations of married life made me feel trapped. I felt numb, overwhelmed, unprepared—and almost claustrophobic. Sure, I had read all the top marriage-prep books. I had endured premarital counseling. But despite how *ready* I felt prior to marriage, the morning after, I felt completely overwhelmed. I have since come to the conclusion that no one—and I mean no one—is prepared for what awaits them in marriage. And this sense of the "new unknown"— the tamed, domestic life—can feel overwhelming.

For some men, this realization hits during their honeymoon. For others it takes a few months. For some men it may even take fifteen to twenty years. But sooner or later every man wakes up to the startling realization that he is in over his head.

Married Bachelor

Last month, a man I'd never met before came into my study and went right to the bottom line: "My name is Ralph and I feel trapped in my marriage." He proceeded to unfold a deep and involved labyrinth of mental and emotional frustration. Unlike some other men seeking marital counsel, he was careful not to blame his wife, but willingly identified his own problems.

"I'm stuck. I feel like there is nowhere to go." He groaned as if his foot were caught in a snare wire. "We have two car payments, two MasterCard receipts, two families to visit on holidays. No matter how hard I try, I'm never satisfied. Do you know what I'm saying? I feel *trapped*." His eyes flashed back and forth across

the room, filled with a desperation. "I thought I knew what I was getting myself into when I got married, but after eleven years, I have to admit I never realized it would turn out like this. I've got to find a way out."

I smiled and assured him he was not the first married man to feel as if he'd bitten off more than he could chew. "There are times every married man feels trapped—because to a certain extent every married man actually *is* trapped."

Now I'm sure that was not exactly the kind of help this man was looking for. In fact, at this point in the conversation I'm sure he was convinced I didn't have both oars in the water.

Since he felt like a trapped animal, I asked him a question to help illustrate his crisis. "Do you know the real difference between a domestic animal and a wild animal?"

His look told me he had no idea how my question was in the least bit relevant to his need. Nonetheless he did a nice job of answering. "A domestic animal learns to submit to the limitations of an owner. A wild animal never does."

"Whether we realize it or not," I proceeded, "the moment a man gets married, he moves from being a wild animal to being a domestic animal. He chooses to be tamed. Before that, we might have been king of the jungle, but the moment we say 'I do' all that changes. If we want the privileges and benefits of marriage, then we also have to accept the fact that we now have to live within the parameters. On the other hand, if we want to roam wild, we have no business *pretending* to fulfill our marriage vows. A domestic animal is one that has learned how to thrive in a new environment."

Ralph chuckled. I could tell by the change in his face and manner that he was experiencing a change in perspective.

"So, what do *you* choose to be?" I asked. "A domestic animal or a wild beast?"

He chuckled again, realizing no one was holding a gun to his head to be a picture-perfect husband. He could walk out on his wife and kids if he wanted, or he could thrive within the parameters. But he could not continue in marriage while secretly longing for the single life.

"I've never thought of it that way!" he said. "Even though

we've been married all these years, something inside of me has been secretly longing to be set free like a wild animal again."

Then Ralph said something I'd never heard before, but it rang with tremendous relevance. "My problem is that I've been a married bachelor. I've nurtured undercover fantasies, thinking that if things didn't work out with my wife I could always move on to another relationship. I guess if I'm going to thrive in my marriage, I need to emotionally close that door and learn how to accept the challenge of my domestic responsibilities. Or, if not, I might as well wad up my marriage license and move on."

A *married bachelor* is indeed an oxymoron. Unfortunately, it's a common mind-set for all too many men. It sounds strange, but some men are their own worst enemies, living at odds with themselves because they never choose to become domestic creatures. Consequently, they're miserable much of their married lives. They continue to believe the wild side of life is where the freedom is, never realizing they're killing themselves—and killing those closest to them in the process.

Wild animals don't survive well in captivity: Married bachelors are always miserable.

Here's what's just as sad as men who walk out: men who stay but never really make peace with their own choice. Married bachelors are men who never make the hard choices, and so they spend their miserable lives complaining about their boundaries and limitations.

Freedom or Frustration

Most men who feel the crushing weight of marital responsibility will want to clear out. It doesn't matter how accomplished we are in work, or how spiritual we think we are. When we feel the great obligation of caring for our wife, we'll instinctively think about running for cover.

I've discovered that many men who feel frustrated in marriage are simply struggling under a sense of being overwhelmed by genuine responsibility. These men are not bums, misfits, or infidels. Most are responsible men who earnestly want to care for their wives but sincerely don't know where to *start*.

Before Ralph left my study, I handed him a 4×6 card and asked him to list the areas in his marriage where he felt overwhelmed. "You need to give me a legal pad," he quipped.

His list was more complete than I expected.

- Financial: "I wish I could provide a better lifestyle."
- Sexual: "I wish I was more stimulating to her."
- Social: "I wish I could initiate more mutual friendships."
- Domestic: "I wish I took better care of the house and yard."
- Parental: "I wish I was a better father, more involved in my kids' lives."
- Spiritual: "I really wish I was a spiritual leader."
- Emotional: "I wish I better understood what makes my wife tick."
- Mental: "I wish I was more challenging to my wife."
- Career: "I wish I personally was challenged by my job."
- Administrative: "I wish I was better organized."

It might sound as if Ralph were suffering from an overdose of inferiority or even despair, but he didn't impress me that way. In fact, I have a hunch that many of us share a great deal in common with him.

I've found that in order to be motivated to be better husbands, most men do not need a kick in the pants. Most men already know they have lots of room for improvement. In fact, many of us see so much room for improvement we're secretly exasperated with ourselves.

Sometimes it seems like crossing the Sahara Desert to travel the distance between where we *are* and where we *want* to be. We don't know where to begin. There are no landmarks. Everything is uncharted. And even if we start the journey, there's no assurance we'll finish alive!

Pathetically, many husbands are walking out of their marriage before they even realize what they got themselves into. In fact, according to *Newsweek,* "a million children a year" watch their fathers walk out the front door. Today, one third of all American children are not living with their natural father.* As we will dis-

---

*Barbara Kantrowitz with Pat Wingert, "Breaking the Divorce Cycle," *Newsweek* (January 13, 1992).

cover, when a man walks away from his home, he is walking away from one of the greatest sources of dignity he could possibly tap into. And deep down most men know it. Most men feel the sour disappointment of divorce in their own gut.

Fortunately, there is another option. When you quite honestly feel like a failure in your own marriage, you may be closer to beginning over than you realize. For some, the sense of failure may be caused by your own self-inflicted, unrealistic standards of excellence. Like Ralph, you may actually be so conscientious in your marriage that you've become a prisoner to your compulsion to please your wife, or to feel good about yourself because of the "super job" you're doing.

If I was to pretend that the only difference between freedom within marriage and frustration within marriage was a mere flick-of-the-switch, I'd be a liar. We know better than to believe in snake oil and quick-fix remedies for complex problems. And so we'll need to tackle the real issues in marriage in the next section.

But first, we need to off-load the false guilt caused by a combination of a hyperactive conscience, a twisted male ego, and a misunderstanding of our wife's expectation. And we can begin by taking a close look at the "myth of the natural-born husband."

Nerds Make Pretty Good Husbands

We are all familiar with the natural-born husband. This is the man with the tidy garage, manicured lawn, and half a dozen well-mannered children. Every month he balances his checkbook, reconciles his credit card statements, and scrubs his wife's white walls. He is active in PTA, church choir, and always gets the best tickets for the major league ball games. His kids are straight-A students and his wife calls him her spiritual leader. For him, nothing is out of place—not a child, not a screwdriver, not a utility bill, and certainly not his temper. He never drinks straight from the milk carton, never loses his breath, and never audibly passes gas. For the natural-born husband, everything in life is right where it belongs.

Stop! We might as well admit it—guys like that drive most of us up the wall.

I have recently come to the conclusion that the natural-born husband is a myth. We might be natural-born athletes, natural-born salesmen, or natural-born leaders. While growing up we exhibit certain raw potential and as men we may have achieved a certain level of success, but when we married, most of us found ourselves strangely out of our element. We fully expected our marriages to hum like well-tuned engines, but for some reason we never thought they would require regular oil changes, lube jobs, or any other form of preventative maintenance. To our bewilderment, rather than building our self-esteem, we discover that our marriages, at least to some extent, are wearing us out. If you're like me, no matter how hard you try, you cannot measure up to your own expectations—especially not those of the woman you married. Perhaps the shining image of the natural-born husband has been beating up on us for too long.

Listen carefully: We were not born with the skills it requires to excel in marriage. We might as well admit that none of us were prepared for marriage. No matter how many books we read, how much premarital counseling we received, or how many seminars we attended, none of us knew what we were getting ourselves into. Every man enters marriage as a rookie, and we are in over our heads from the minute we say "I do."

> ## The sooner we recognize that we are not "natural-born" husbands, the sooner we can begin to develop some much needed marital skills.

The natural-born husband may be found somewhere in Greek mythology and he may even thrive in old TV sitcoms, but he can't breathe for long in the harsh atmosphere of real life. Pretty soon, any guy who tries to be "the perfect husband" is going to crash and burn.

Feeling Like a Loser

When Howard and Patty came into my office, it didn't take long to realize that Howard felt like a failure. He wouldn't look me in the eyes, and his slumped posture was the picture of helplessness. Neither of them was able to understand the other's perspective, accusations were flying. Patty was expressing her frustration because Howard seemed so unmotivated, and Howard made it clear he was sick and tired of being told what to do. Many words were fired into the air, and no healthy communication was taking place.

In the course of this fire fight, I noticed that crawling around inside Howard was a hurting, dejected person. If he had been in there all along, it was no wonder she was frustrated. What woman, who escorts her man to the altar, wants to wake up one day to find herself in bed with a little boy? I asked him, "Would you please tell Patty how you feel about yourself?"

He looked at me with shock. Patty turned to look at him as if to say, *This should be interesting.*

Howard's head hung down like a whipped dog. "I feel like a loser. I feel like I can't do anything right. No matter what I try, it doesn't work out." He was finally expressing his frustration in words that made sense. Immediately, Patty was touched, and she reached over to squeeze his hand. But he withdrew his hand quickly, and his voice cracked. "I just can't take any more."

After some quiet moments, I asked, "When did you start to feel this way?"

"Ever since I lost my job," Howard said in a rush of emotion, "nothing has worked out. I had high expectations for myself, but nothing's gone according to schedule."

In the next twenty minutes, Howard expressed things he had never verbalized before, opening for Patty a whole new world of her husband's inner life—thoughts, feelings, and harsh self-judgments that she didn't know existed. Howard knew his wife was raised in a family where the nicer things in life came easy, and he knew their poverty-level income was definitely substandard. When Howard failed to bring home the big bucks, he felt that he was a failure as a man. Because he felt like a loser in Patty's eyes, he was venting his frustrations back at her. He was mistakenly seeing her as the source of his bad feelings, rather than his own self-criticism. No wonder Patty was thoroughly confused! As we talked through this process, they not only began to understand each other, it appeared they were willing for reconciliation. A big step.

I then asked Patty, "When you were married, were you ready to commit yourself to Howard?"

"Oh yes. That's what I wanted. I trusted Howard. I believed in him. I still do, but I'm confused."

"Why? What happened?"

"I still *want* to believe in him," she said thoughtfully, "but it's harder now that he doesn't believe in himself."

Bingo! Patty had landed on the bedrock of Howard's soul. It is very difficult to believe in the leadership of anyone who doesn't believe in himself. It's hard to consistently treat with honor and deference people who themselves project a lack of confidence and dignity.

"Howard," I said, turning to him, "did you hear what your wife just said? She is ready to affirm your leadership—to follow your lead. She believed in you when you were first married, and she wants to believe in you now."

For the first time, Howard squared his shoulders and looked Patty in the face. They locked eyes, and smiled. Though this level of mutual understanding was new to both of them, it obviously felt good. As he looked back at me, his eyes had lost their gray, dull look of failure. I saw a flicker of hope and dignity rekindled.

When Howard owned up to his failure in front of Patty, a heavy load seemed to slide from his shoulders; it was as if he was set free from the myth of the natural-born husband. I will never forget the next statement Howard expressed. Looking his wife in her face he said, "Honey, do you mean it's okay if I blow it once in a while?" They hugged. They felt a new level of dignity. Patty was expressing to Howard that she would rather have a husband with a sensitive heart than a six-figure income. They were certainly not wallowing in their failure, but they were accepting and understanding each other for the first time in months.

As Howard and Patty walked from my study that day, I realized they were walking out into a world where they were not unique. Thousands of other couples share a similar struggle as they wrestle with failure in one area of life that seems to add an unbearable weight to an already unhealthy marriage. When men face failure in business, it is doubly hard for them to face failure in marriage. The element that is most needed in such situations is the willingness to lay aside the unrealistic expectation of perfection, including the myth of the natural-born husband.

Howard's problem with his wife actually turned out to be Howard's problem with himself. He was trapped by his own image of the natural-born husband so that it kept him from being the man he really was. Once he took off the costume and came out from hiding, his wife once again had a husband and he had the self-worth that comes from being true to himself.

Successful Failure

Those who fail at business are not the only ones who find it difficult admitting they are failing at marriage. Sometimes those who succeed at business find it even more difficult to claim their rookie status in marriage.

A highly successful young real estate broker in metro Atlanta recently shared with me that eight months ago he was ready to walk out on his wife. "I thought establishing my career and being successful in sales would be the toughest challenge of my life. So when I graduated from college, that's where I placed my shots. Now I see that my career was relatively easy compared to making my marriage work and being able to communicate with my children. At work I dictate a memo and everything gets done; I send a fax and I know it gets through. Yet I drive only twenty minutes to my home and suddenly all the rules change. Why is it that I can relate so effectively with my colleagues who are not really important to me, and yet I can't communicate easily with my wife and children, who mean everything in the world to me?"

That afternoon as my realtor friend and I shared a lunch together, we discussed one of the vital dynamics of marriage—coming to the humble realization that although I might be a smashing success at certain areas of life, at the same moment I might be failing miserably at marriage. One of the hardest things in the world is to walk out of a banquet where we've been honored as the top salesman of the year or the top professor or the top anything and then drive home to eat a plate full of humble pie. For some men that is too much to swallow.

- It's tough being told we're lousy at managing the family budget when we are honored for managing a budget fifty times that size at work.

- It's rough being told by our spouse we're insensitive, when our secretary tells everyone how kind and considerate we are.
- It hurts when our wives complain about the yard and gutters, when we run an efficient business that spins like a top.

Perfectionism

For those of us who feel like failures in the home while we are succeeding elsewhere, there is bad news and good news. The bad news is that none of us were born with what it requires to be a perfect husband; the good news is that deep down inside, your wife really doesn't want to be married to a perfect husband anyway.

Just think about it. In order for your wife to be married to a perfect husband, it would mean she would be expected to be a perfect wife. What horrifying pressure that would place her under! No woman in her right mind wants the stress of being required to be a perfect wife. Fortunately, perfectionism is not on any husband's job description either. Rather, it is a myth that must be burned in effigy.

Believe it or not, most wives have far more realistic expectations for their husbands than their husbands have for themselves.

Sally was a drop-dead beautiful woman, yet she was in the process of securing a divorce and deeply regretting it. When she told me her story, I listened carefully, but it was painful to hear. That day she told me something I have never forgotten.

"George and I were high school sweethearts. He was the star quarterback on the football team and I was the captain of the cheerleaders and homecoming queen. We were both popular and appeared to be the perfect couple. I thought he was Prince Charming and as far as I know he saw me as his fair princess. We were very much in love with each other and blind to what it would require to make our marriage work. When it came to giving of ourselves, we didn't have a clue. When we got married everything seemed to change; the fantasy was over. Bills piled up; then I got pregnant. Discovering reality was like hitting a brick wall. We exchanged our name brand clothes for diapers, and instead of dancing, partying, and running around on weekends, we were stuck at home with nowhere to go. The things I had admired in him seemed to wear thin, and the qualities I would now look for in a husband have changed radically." Then she said one of those classic statements that I found profoundly insightful. "I would now be happy to be married to the class nerd; at least he would treat me with respect."

Did you hear what she said? This drop-dead beautiful woman said that she would happily have been married to the class nerd. When she first made that statement, I could not believe my ears, but I have since heard dozens of women say something similar. It seems that the "pre-married profile" on what makes for a good spouse quickly changes once we say "I do." Obviously, her point was not to suggest that all nerds make great life partners. Nor was she saying a good husband is a nerd. What she was saying is this: Marriage is not based on outward attraction—popularity, muscles, brains, money. Rather, marriage grows out of the inner qualities that are often overlooked in courtship. What it requires to start a romantic fire is not what keeps it burning.

Expectations

The pre-married profile of what makes a great husband is often temporal and superficial—almost faddish. This is a typical list of what collegiate co-eds look for in a man:

- Stylish dresser
- Handsome
- Sense of humor
- Hot car
- Good kisser
- Spends money
- Self-confident/cocky
- Laid-back/carefree

Once the vows are taken and real life gets started, the list of what women desire in their husbands often changes dramatically. Few, if any, of the previous characteristics carry over into marriage. Once sharing an apartment, paying utility bills, doing dishes, balancing budgets, cleaning vomit stains and all the rest kick into gear, there is an entirely new list of characteristics women look for in their spouses.

- Patience
- Manners, politeness
- Compliments
- Sensitivity
- Thoughtfulness
- Compassion
- Saves money
- Words of affection
- Responsibility
- Organization
- A homebody

A factor that accentuates this problem is that most wives do not adequately tell us that their profile has changed. As men we remember watching our wife's eyes light up when we drove up in the hot car and bought her expensive gifts. Rarely does a woman flat out sit her husband down and explain that the list of qualities she admires has radically changed. It's no wonder we are often left scratching our heads.

Image

Long-haired, flamboyant tennis superstar Andre Agassi spins around, cocks his head, looks over the rim of his jet-black sunglasses and says in his Joe Cool voice, "Image is everything!" That may be a catchy advertising slogan that motivates the sale of 35-millimeter cameras, but it's paper-thin marital advice. In marriage, image is not everything. In fact, it's more accurate to say, "Image isn't anything." Image may have been a dating concern, but in marriage it's a definite liability. The faster we can get beyond the prideful superficiality of image, the sooner the depth of our marriage relationship can begin to develop honestly and compassionately.

Maintaining our high school or college image can be one of

the most destructive influences in marriage. Without realizing it we may be keeping our wives at arms' length. Image is a projection of who we would like to be but are not. As long as we are projecting an image, no one—not even those closest to us—will be able to get to know who we really are. Just as a butterfly breaks out of a chrysalis and a newly hatched bird breaks from its shell, there comes a time when we must grow out of the games we used to play in order to attract the opposite sex. Once we are married, the qualities that had previously attracted the opposite sex will possibly become the very same qualities that now become repulsive to our wives.

We may hate to admit it, but nerds make potentially good husbands.

Don't worry. We will not go off the deep end with this thought, but it is worth arm wrestling with a moment longer. Obviously, it doesn't mean that we would all be better off if we were ugly, uncoordinated, under-achieving men. However, the real qualities our wives are waiting to see in us have probably changed radically from our dating days.

> # There is nothing that drives our wives away from us faster than our little ego trips.

Off With the Armor

While we devote the next chapter to the destructive effects of the twisted male ego, we need to make certain observations right now. Prior to marriage some of us put a great deal of energy into the competitive little ego games we played to impress each other. We always wanted to look our best, smell our best, sound our best, and be our best; consequently, we related to each other strength to strength. This stage in the development of our relationships is a safe, rewarding, self-fulfilling level where we feel very much in control. Probably 99% of all relationships begin at this level, and that's normal—as far as superficial relationships go. After all, we would never pursue a relationship if we were not positively attracted to each other. If a relationship never moves beyond the point of strength-to-strength attraction, however, it will only remain superficial. In fact, any relationship that continues on a merely strength-to-strength attraction basis will soon self-destruct, because two unchecked egos will always lock horns. These forces that began as attraction points will actually become points of rivalry. In order for our marriages to mature, the partners not only need to take off the costume of perfectionism but they also need to be willing to show to each other their dark sides and weaknesses. Prince Charming obviously can't sleep with his armor on, and even the fair princess needs to shave her legs.

Admittedly, the first time we take off the armor, we will feel a level of insecurity and vulnerability. Our inclination will be to put it right back on again. But be assured that your wife does not want a plastic-coated husband; she wants an authentic man who is mature enough to express his own failures and shortcomings. And rest assured, it won't take long until we appreciate how much more comfortable life is without wearing the heavy armor.

As we take off our armor, we might as well go ahead and lay aside our prejudices against some of the softer, inner qualities of manhood—manners, compliments, patience, sensitivity, compassion, forgiveness, and humility. While the whole myth of the natural-born husband is rooted in pride and superficiality, our wives are actually longing for us to develop the inner character of genuine manliness. And even if they are not asking for it, you can be sure they'll recognize it when they see it.

The comic strip Pogo made a profound admission that often applies to men in marriage: "We met the enemy, and they is us." Fasten your seat belts. We are about to investigate our greatest, secret, silent enemy—the male ego.

Our Secret Enemy

Any book for men that avoids the issue of destructive pride is not worth reading. Twisted pride is the greatest single enemy of any relationship, particularly our most intimate one. Pride does more than simply compete for attention—it fights to the kill. It craves center stage, claws to the top of the pile, screams for attention, manipulates for control, and becomes utterly irrational and vicious in its quest for dominion. There is nothing that is as repulsive to our wives and nothing that is as invisible to ourselves as our own pride.

A Lesson From a Ski Boat

It was a beautiful day in south Florida. I was driving a speed boat and my wife was jumping waves on a slalom ski behind us. "Wow! She is terrific!" my friend shouted. "I've never seen anyone ski like that before! She could get a job at Cypress Gardens!" At first his words evoked a level of joyful pride in my heart. *"Yeah! And to think—she's my wife!"* I told myself.

As she pulled herself into the boat and reached for a towel, Sherry looked at me and announced, "Now it's your turn!" With these words my tide of emotion shifted, and I suddenly felt something strange inside—intimidation.

Normally, athletics come very naturally to me, but I had only

water-skied one time in my life, and I had never before slalomed. *C'mon, you've just seen such an impressive demonstration,* I reasoned. *You can't let her show you up.* So I put on my life vest, grabbed a ski, and jumped into the water with an unrealistically high level of self-confidence. *Piece of cake!* I tried to convince myself even though deep down I knew better.

My ski was in position, the rope was tight. I yelled, "Hit it!" The 150-horsepower outboard gave my dead weight a noble effort, but I definitely did not pop up out of the water as fluently as Sherry did. In fact, I lunged headfirst, lost my ski in the process, and finally let go of the rope before I dredged the lake bottom with my body.

As the boat drove slowly around me, allowing me to grab the rope for a second time, my friend yelled, "No big deal. We'll try again. You'll make it this time."

I did indeed try again . . . and again, and again, and again. Finally they tossed me another ski, hoping I could at least get up on two. I overheard my friend ask, "Fred hasn't skied before, has he?"

"I guess not," Sherry answered. "But he sure tries hard."

Small condolence for my bruised ego.

This time I had no problems getting up, but for some reason skiing on two skis after watching my wife tear it up on one was not terribly fulfilling. As I bounced across the waves, I felt like a little boy using training wheels.

I climbed back in the boat and resumed driving. This time before I even had a chance to lick my badly bruised ego, Sherry jumped back in the water, put on her short trick skis and gave us a demonstration of skiing backward and doing three-sixties. Her private ski show climaxed by dropping one trick ski while skiing backward. "Awesome! Look at her go backward on one ski!" my friend swooned.

I had to agree she was impressive, whether I wanted to or not.

What happened to me that day behind the ski boat is a microcosm of what is common to every marriage. At the time I would not have admitted to it. In fact, at the time I was hardly aware of the dynamic that I was experiencing internally. But the fact remains that I was suffering an ego crisis. Because my pride was injured, my weakness was not capable of rejoicing in her strength. This same process is repeated thousands of times every day.

- Phil tells me, "I can't stand it! My wife told me to sell my Chrysler stock and I didn't listen to her. Then it dropped *fifteen* points—and I never hear the end of it."
- John says, "All my wife talks about is her parents. How they prayed together and talked together and worked together and never got in an argument. The family I grew up in was so different. All this talk about her parents makes me sick."
- Jim writes, "I don't know what to do. My wife is Miss Prim and Proper. For her, everything needs to be in its place and she lets me know when it's not. She complains about my laundry, my dental floss, my tools, my receipts, my manners, my hair, my everything. As far as I'm concerned she can just take her etiquette and get out of my face!"

These men have at least one thing in common: Each guy is married to a woman who has a strength that exposes an area of his weakness. Rather than benefiting from their spouses' strengths, they are recoiling in self-defense.

And there is another factor that makes these relationships more tricky.

Meeting Our Match

In marriage our pride comes up against an equally diabolic force—our spouse's ego. Our pride instinctively knows that it cannot share territorial rights, and the boundaries where these two territories meet is the ground where we collide and sparks begin to fly. Pride, by definition, demands preeminence. Therefore, when two people, each with independent egos, seek to co-exist without some predetermined means of dealing with their own pride issues, they will sooner or later seek to dominate or destroy. Forget the fact that the two individuals may love each other. Forget the fact that they may have children they'd give their lives for. Forget the fact that if they walked down the street and spotted each other in the crowd, they would still find themselves very much attracted to each other. Forget the fact that most likely if this couple gets a divorce, both will marry a new partner who is not unlike their current spouse. When egos lock horns nothing else matters. There is no rational explanation left for the hideous ways two adults treat each other once they start into the dominate-or-destroy mode.

No one has done a better job analyzing this insidious force than C. S. Lewis in his classic *Mere Christianity*. Even if you've read this excerpt before, read it now with your marriage in mind.

> There is one vice of which no man in the world is free; which every one in the world loathes when he sees it in someone else; and of which hardly any people, except Christians, ever imagine that they are guilty themselves. . . .
>
> The vice I am talking of is Pride or Self-Conceit: and the virtue opposite to it, in Christian morals, is called Humility . . . the essential vice, the utmost evil is Pride. Unchastity, anger, greed, drunkenness, and all that, are mere flea bites in comparison: it was through Pride that the devil became the devil: Pride leads to every other vice: it is the complete anti-God state of mind. . . .
>
> If you want to find out how proud you are, the easiest way is to ask yourself, "How much do I dislike it when other people snub me, or refuse to take any notice of me, or shove their oar in, or patronize me, or show off?" The point is that each person's pride is in competition with every one else's pride. It is because I wanted to be the big noise at the party that I am so annoyed at someone else being the big noise. Two of a trade never agree. Now what you want to get clear is that Pride is essentially competitive—is competitive by its very nature—while the other vices are competitive only, so to speak, by accident. Pride gets no pleasure out of having something, only out of having more of it than the next man. We say that people are proud of being rich, or clever, or good-looking, but they are not. They are proud of being richer, or cleverer, or better-looking than others. If every one else became equally rich, or clever, or good-looking there would be nothing to be proud about. It is the comparison that makes you proud: the pleasure of being above

the rest. Once the element of competition has gone, pride has gone. That is why I say that Pride is essentially competitive in a way that other vices are not. . . .

It is Pride which has been the chief cause of misery in every nation and every family since the world began. Other vices may sometimes bring people together: you may find good fellowship and jokes and friendliness among drunken people or unchaste people. But pride always means enmity— it is enmity. And not only enmity between man and man, but enmity to God.

In God you come up against something which is in every respect immeasurably superior to yourself. Unless you know God as that—and, therefore, know yourself as nothing in comparison—you do not know God at all. As long as you are proud, you cannot know God. A proud man is always looking down on things and people: and, of course, as long as you are looking down, you cannot see something that is above you.*

Healthy/Unhealthy

It needs to be said at this point that not all pride is bad. When Isaiah Thomas's mother hugged him courtside after the Detroit Pistons won the NBA Championship and he was chosen Most Valuable Player, she sighed, "Son, I'm so proud . . . so proud." Such a spontaneous expression of genuine admiration and delight is perfectly healthy and appropriate. Healthy pride is what we refer to as *dignity*.

Similarly, my children gave me a bright red T-shirt last Father's Day that reads, "Greatest Dad On Earth." At first I was a little self-conscious wearing it in public until my wife suggested, "If you bought it for yourself; that would be unhealthy pride. But since your children bought it for you, it would be unhealthy not to wear it." Dignity is what I feel wearing that T-shirt.

Dignity, or healthy pride, has a significant role in each of our

*Reprinted by permission from *Mere Christianity* by C.S. Lewis, published by Harper-Collins Publishers Limited.

lives. It is a source of positive motivation and it provides us with a deep sense of genuine fulfillment. Unhealthy pride, however, is a most destructive motivation that pushes a man to excess, flaws his judgment, and provokes him to even attack that which he knows is sacred.

At times we use the same word to describe both attitudes, but they are light years apart. In fact, it is fair to say that until we learn to put away a destructive pride, we will never learn how to savor the delight of dignity. To put that another way—the key to true dignity as a man is to learn to put away our destructive male egos.

As we learn to discern the difference between the two, it may be helpful to consider how they contrast with each other by setting the two side by side:

Unhealthy Pride	Dignity (Healthy Pride)
To gain self-satisfaction by getting my way.	To gain inner fulfillment by effectively completing my responsibilites.
The inner drive to serve my own self-interests.	The desire to serve others in the duties of life.
Craving for my own personal advancement.	Enjoying and contributing to the success of others.
Thinking I have no one to thank but myself for my achievements.	Realizing that God and others are to be credited in my success.
My goal is to be the greatest and to have others serve me.	I want to be the best I can be at serving others.
I am my only boss and the master of my destiny.	I am a man under authority and live within the providence of God, serving God by serving my boss.
To project an image of perfection.	To honestly face my imperfections.

A Head-On Collision

The irony of conflicting egos is that, in part, marriage was designed to bring two egos together. Selfish pride will always be exposed in a marriage, because it comes into contact with the equally selfish nature of our spouse. When we enter into marriage, it is more than a cliche to say, "I've met my match." Indeed, my ego has met its match in my wife's ego. The problem is, few men were given any preparation in how to negotiate the head-on collision.

Right now, it may well be that you are face-to-face for the first time with a decision that will alter the rest of your life. Maybe you have never seen that your ego is exposed by locking horns with your wife's ego. Rather than continuing to destroy an otherwise good marriage, you can start to make some mature choices. Your marriage can become the very environment it was intended to be—the place where your destructive pride is itself transformed into godly humility.

When we allow our selfish ego to be removed, we are free to find the fullness of our true dignity.

Mature Choices

Marriage calls us toward maturity. It encourages us to grow up, assume responsibility for our own actions, and to confront the self-destructive pride within. Marriage does not create ego problems; rather, it reveals ego problems that have existed all along but have never before been exposed. To blame our spouses for all our internal conflicts is cowardly and childish. To walk away from marriages because we have locked horns at a deeply frustrating level means that we are walking away from maturity. We will either walk into other relationships where we will need to confront the same destructive ego or we may choose to never grow up.

I wonder how many men walk out of marriage because deep down they just don't want to face themselves. I suppose there are those who sacrifice true dignity on the altar of their self-destructive egos—men who pout and strut and manipulate and abuse and play silly high-school games, who never assume responsibility for all the head-butting. How sad that the one ultimate element every man longs for—dignity—is the one prize that will always elude the blind egotist.

Marriage requires maturity because marriage requires us to *love*. True love only grows out of genuine humility.

Back to the Ski Boat

True, clashing with my wife's athletic skills seems like a light-weight example of destructive pride. But for me, water-skiing became a very positive paradigm. In this relatively safe, innocuous area of our marriage, I was first able to confront my pride head on. It was ugly, obnoxious—and it puts up a good fight! It was intent on destroying the dignity my wife received from her expertise. But I saw its plan and did not allow it to run its course. I deliberately chose to humble myself, and I learned several vital insights that have been helpful in countless other areas of our relationship:

- Now I can applaud my wife's strength without competing with it or attempting to destroy it.
- I can delight in her skill for what it is and affirm her dignity.
- I can enjoy my level of ability in a certain area without comparing myself to her.
- Together we can help each other develop to the best of our potential.

You may ask, "Do you enjoy water-skiing today?" A little bit. "Are you any better at the sport than you were nineteen years ago?" Not considerably. But every year I make sure Sherry gets to ski just so I can watch her enjoy her tremendous talent in this area. In a sense, I enjoy water-skiing vicariously by simply admiring her gracefully cut across the surface. And when I get a chance to ski, I must admit it is now much easier and more fun without the anvil of pride strapped to my back!

The "ski boat" of your marriage may be any number of things:

- Your wife's organizational skills
- Her intellect
- The lifestyle of your in-laws
- Her spirituality

- Her friendships or social life
- Her successful career
- Her skill at backgammon
- Whatever!

Any area of life where our spouse's strengths threaten us qualifies as a ski boat. The important question to ask in ski-boat situations is not, "Who is the best skier?" or "Who has the greatest strength in this area?" Rather, the critical question is always, "Am I willing to let my wife's strengths shine?" Period.

We will return to this critical area several times before we are done. Now we need to look at one creative way to rid ourselves of our destructive pride.

How to Win Your Wife's Affection

The most basic task of any married man is to live in such a way that his wife knows she is the most important person in his world. Choosing to honor her for her strengths is the first, major step in accomplishing this task. Keeping her convinced is another task we will save for our next section. Now we want to focus on winning her affection initially.

Once we stop locking horns, how do we convince her of her central place in our lives? When we learn this lesson, we win not only our wife's affection but her trust, loyalty, support, devotion, and admiration. In short, we can lay down the weight of false pride and terrible competition with our wife, and with the flood of new emotional support you will rediscover dignity.

"I Object"

I can almost hear an objection. "Hey, who says I need to win anything from my wife? I'm already married, right? I don't need to *earn* anything—she owes it to me." This objection reminds me of Peter.

Peter and I played on the same slow-pitch softball team. After the game one afternoon he asked if we could talk. "I've been married two years, and it keeps getting worse and worse. They told me it would get better after the first year but it hasn't. I'm sick of it. I don't know how much more I can take. All she does is complain all the time."

Peter proceeded to spread out the long list of his wife's grievances.

- "All you want is five minutes of sex—you make me feel like a prostitute."
- "You are always out drinking with your friends, spending our money."
- "You talk so mean and nasty—I'm like your slave."
- "I have a long list of chores you never get done."
- "We never talk with each other—you just sit around and watch TV."
- "I'm afraid of you—when your temper explodes I withdraw, and I'm scared to come out of my shell."
- "If this continues I'm going back to live with my mother."
- "You need to get some help."

I was impressed with how well Peter listened to his wife, and I told him so. "Usually it goes in one ear and out the other. Some men don't have any idea what their wives are saying. At least you are off to a good start."

It became obvious in the course of our conversation that Peter's aggressive personality was killing his marriage, and he didn't even know it. Being compulsive-aggressive was an asset as the shortstop on our softball team and in his job as a building contractor, but it was a severe liability to his marriage.

As Peter and I sat in the cool of a shade tree discussing his woes, he burst out, "Hey, who says I need to win anything from my wife? We're already married. She owes it to me." He was looking at me with fire in his eyes, his jaw tight, and his eyebrows fiercely furrowed, as if he were about to throw me out at second base. I could see why his wife would be intimidated.

But underneath, I saw a young man who was thoroughly confused and begging for answers. For the next hour we rationally discussed a perspective he never previously considered—we talked about how to win his wife's affection.

Easter Chicks

As we sat there in the shade, Peter was carefully weighing the issues. "I sure love her," he reflected. "But," he added, "at other times she makes me so angry I could kill her." If I'd had a voltage meter, I know his level of intensity would register consistently in the red.

"Peter, perhaps you *are* killing her," I interjected. He looked at me as if I were nuts. "No. Hang on, I'm serious. You may be killing her. You are so possessive and compulsive in your behavior, you're probably in the process of killing any trust she ever had in you. And you don't even realize it."

To illustrate my point, I told Peter about the newborn Easter chicks my parents gave me when I was four or five years old. These tiny yellow puffs of fluffy feathers could barely stand up and peep. We kept them alive with a single lightbulb, covered with a blanket in a cardboard box. "They were so cute and lovable I couldn't keep my hands off them. I held them, cradled them, cuddled them, and squeezed them. In fact, I cuddled one of the chicks so tightly and so much, it died. Without being aware, I'd suffocated the very thing I loved."

It is easier than we realize to kill the object of our love. Peter seemed to understand.

There is a time for love to be hands-on, and there is a time for love to be hands-off. Wives thrive on a proper balance, but their affection is easily suffocated if we administer inappropriate doses of either. One of the marital skills we all need to learn is when to be hands-on and when to be hands-off. Our inclination is often to flip-flop.

Peter was hands-off when his wife wanted him hands-on.

- He neglected their lawn and yard care.
- The house needed painting.
- He never balanced the check book.
- The bills piled up for months.
- He never went to church with her.

And he was hands-on when she wanted him hands-off.

- He manipulated her emotions.

- He wouldn't allow her to visit her mother.
- The moment he heard her bra strap pop open in the bedroom at night, he demanded gratification.
- He was extremely jealous and would ask countless questions about every detail of every conversation she'd had all day long.

As we talked, I assured Peter I did not question his love for his wife—but his manner of expressing love was suspect. Needless to say, his wife was unimpressed.

Peter, like most men, thought his marriage was a done deal and that his wife's affections were a guaranteed part of the agreement—almost the "blow-in-my-ear-and-I'll-follow-you-anywhere" approval. But women are not machines that respond at the flick of a switch. And as most of us have already discovered, they will not hesitate to remind us of that fact.

For those of us who are prone toward being compulsive-aggressive husbands—and for those who simply get lazy from time to time—there is only one solution that will keep us from eventually killing our wives' affection and trust. It's what I call "the 100% principle." I first considered it while taking a long walk on the beach.

A Walk on the Beach

I could relate to Peter's confession. I've already mentioned the ton of emotional bricks that fell on me the first morning after our wedding. It got worse before it got better. Our first year of marriage was a near disaster, and my wedding vows were severely tested. Growing up, there was one thing I really hated —watching my mother cry. When I got married, I discovered a second thing that was equally disturbing—watching my wife cry. During our first year of marriage, Sherry must have cried a hundred times. It was gruesome, for her and for me. At first I tried to hide behind a long list of carefully crafted excuses.

Oh, she's just too emotional.
It's her monthly cycle.
She's spoiled.
She's trying to manipulate me.

She just wants to eat out every night.
She was just raised with a silver spoon in her mouth.
She's being immature.
She's just overly sensitive.

My list went on and on. Her emotional mood swings certainly had me baffled, and I needed to blame it on something. I pretended to understand her hurts and alleviate her sorrows, but deep down I had a hunch the problem was more hers than mine. Even my efforts to help her were token.

After all, I had strutted into marriage thinking I was the greatest thing that could have happened in my wife's life. I always considered myself an expert at impressing girls and therefore thought I would have no difficulty keeping Sherry impressed—with my wit, my humor, my personality, my athletic skills, my style, my looks, my money, my charm. This sounds warped, but I was so impressed with myself I couldn't imagine why my wife was not more impressed. It didn't take long for our honeymoon high to run out of gas and come crashing to earth like a lead balloon. Not only was she unimpressed, she was actually depressed. That I could not understand.

I can't remember the topic, but I can certainly remember the effect—one afternoon we locked horns. We had been married only one month, still living on a secluded island with miles of beaches, tropical climate, few cares, fine restaurants and more recreational facilities than we had time to utilize. Yet we locked horns and our attitudes froze up. We were both offended and nothing seemed to help. We tried talking, we tried playing tennis, we tried walking, we tried jogging, we tried praying. For a moment it seemed that even God was unable to find a solution to our spat.

I needed some space to let my mind air out, so that evening I went for a walk along the beach in the moonlight. I was deeply troubled and was unable to regain my own equilibrium. All alone and with the cool sand pressing through my toes, a concept so terrifying and radical walked across my mind that my mouth got dry and my palms began to sweat. I was desperate and needed help, but I assure you that when I first sifted these words through the logic-organizer of my mind, the thoughts came at me like a night-stalker:

> *From now on, any problem you and Sherry have in your marriage is primarily your problem.*

Every time those words replayed in my brain, I argued with them.

> *That can't be right.*
> *It's not fair.*
> *She'll take advantage of me.*
> *I can't assume responsibility for all our problems. She'll never grow up.*
> *I have to wear the pants in the family.*

After blowing off steam, I became convinced that that command, which so deeply troubled me, could not have been generated from my own imagination; perhaps they originated with God, as a sort of "let's get to the bottom line" type of answer to my prayer for help. But as to the logic of it—well, it was certainly on a level higher than anything I'd previously considered. In fact, emotionally, I was still engaged in spitting and sputtering, and so what came next hit me hard, as if God had decided it was time to use the jackhammer:

> *Don't ever complain to me about Sherry's problems. Any of the problems she's dealing with are now problems you must help her with. You are not responsible for her, but you are responsible to her. She does not need you rubbing her face in her faults any longer. Rather than sitting in judgment over her, you must come alongside her and be her friend.*

As these thoughts began to take hold, I could discern that something major was altering my life and my perspective. And I knew that if I was going to take this advice seriously, I would no longer reserve the right to piously stand back and silently scold my wife with an attitude that said, *"You jerk! When will you ever grow up!?! Why can't you see things the way I do? Obviously I'm right and you're wrong."* It was threatening for me to consider laying down all my hoarded artillery. My self-preserving instincts were rebelling. This would be like trekking into hostile territory unprotected. Nevertheless, something deep inside was convincing me that I was moving in the proper direction.

I didn't realize it at the time, but I was getting my first lesson in what it means to employ the 100% principle in marriage.

Perhaps the easiest way to explain the 100% principle is to compare it to something we all know pretty well—the principle of "give and take."

"You scratch my back and I'll scratch yours."
"I'll meet you halfway."
"You owe me a favor."
"It's your turn next time."

Fifty-one Percent

The marriage concept of "give and take" seems so reasonable, so relational. And though it might sound harmless, it has actually destroyed more marriages than all the whore houses in history.

Sometime ago, as I approached the cash register at a local convenience store, the latest gossip newspaper caught my eye. It was the type of tabloid that ordinarily flaunts articles on UFOs, three-headed babies, and the latest rock-star romance. I can assure you that I am not in the habit of reading such publications, but scanning the front covers as I wait my turn in line frequently gives me a grin. This particular issue featured a photo of Elizabeth Taylor and her then-newlywed husband, U.S. Senator John Warner from Virginia. Alongside their picture in bold print was the announcement:

We've learned the secret to marriage.

This should be a good one, I snorted. To satisfy my curiosity I read the fine print and discovered Miss Taylor's "innovative" idea.

"John and I have learned the secret of marriage—we both give 51%."

I did not need any great prophetic powers to predict that Miss Taylor's marriage would not last long. Sadly, it didn't.

Now 51% sounds marginally superior to the standard 50–50%, but it is still based on the same underlying "give-and-take" concept that dominates most modern marriages. Just think: If on a good day the husband gives 51% and the wife also concedes 51%, there will be, *at best,* a 2% overlap. This also means that if one spouse wakes up in the morning feeling a little shabby and decides to give only 48%, they have already begun to separate and build a gulf between them.

Vows

We better not snicker too loudly at Miss Taylor's concept because many of us with high intentions have been using a similar form of percentage plan. If it is not 50–50% or 51–51%, maybe it's 75–75% or even 90–90%.

As a pastor of a young congregation in northeast metro-Atlanta, I preside over a number of weddings every year. They rank among my happiest pastoral duties. When I stand in my formal garb facing the beaming bride and groom and a room full of witnesses, I recite vows to which the couple verbally agrees. The vows are a vital element to any wedding ceremony. They form the substance of the wedding covenant and they usually include some variation on the traditional phrases.

> . . . to have and to hold
> from this day forward,
> for better, for worse,
> for richer, for poorer,
> in sickness and in health,
> to love and to cherish
> till death do us part.

These vows—and virtually all wedding vows, regardless how

unique or creative they might be—do not represent any form of the percentage plan, not even a 90–90% plan. Though it may not be stated explicitly, wedding vows implicitly call for 100% commitment. When the bride and groom make their pledge, it is generally understood they are making to each other a total commitment.

Nowhere does the marriage covenant state that the commitment will be fulfilled so long as certain conditions are met. The vows include no loopholes, fine print, or exemption clauses: Marriage vows are unconditional. To state this more explicitly, marriage vows are not based on a give-and-take principle. They do not say:

- "I will continue to love you as long as you love me."
- "I will remain morally faithful to you as long as you are loyal to me."
- "I will take care of you when you are sick as long as you don't get too sick."

Such statements represent a shallow level of commitment and would therefore not be included in the vows, because marriage is not meant to be shallow. While our vows may not include such statements, however, these conditional clauses often become our unwritten code of conduct. All too easily we vow total commitment on our wedding day, but we live *partial* commitment from then on. It seems as if we add footnotes to the marriage contract that might include any number of escape hatches.

- . . . except if she snores.
- . . . not if she gains twenty pounds.
- . . . unless she spends too much money.
- . . . as long as she treats me with respect.
- . . . until I don't "feel in love" with her anymore.

No, I have never heard these words mentioned at a wedding, but apparently they are silently tucked away in the subway system of our hearts like stowaways of selfishness. At first such thoughts appear harmless because newlyweds rarely anticipate their vows being tested. Then when the marital pressures start rising, these escape clauses begin to crawl out of hiding.

Fact: Every marriage vow will be tested.

If we maintain a percentage-plan approach to marriage, our marriage will maintain the inverse level of risk—i.e., if we follow a 70–70% plan, we will be living on a 30% risk factor.

Our Role Model

Peter, my softball buddy, had listened carefully as I related my early discoveries about marriage and my self-centeredness. It was now nearing sundown, and I could tell he was thinking seriously about the price he'd need to pay if he chose to enter into a 100% commitment to his wife.

I reached in my Nike bag and pulled out a small Bible I carry with me, more like a heavenly *Walkman* than a good-luck charm. It's a book I can read on the fly for inspiration or instruction. I was motivated to read Peter a verse that had exploded inside of me the night I took a walk on the beach one month into my marriage.

"Get ready," I forewarned Peter, as if tossing him a hand grenade:

> "Husbands, love your wives, just as Christ loved the church and gave himself up for her" (Ephesians 5:21).

Trying desperately not to sound "preachy," I still needed to give at least a light dose of commentary. So I reminded Peter of the strategy Jesus used when He set out to win the loyalty of His followers, and how effective His style of leadership has been. Any rag-tag theologian knows that the final events of Jesus' life were not pretty. He was personally betrayed, verbally mocked, falsely accused, unjustly convicted, physically beaten, socially humiliated, emotionally battered, and brutally executed in a most gruesome manner—by crucifixion. And yet, all of this ugly treatment reveals one fact: Jesus modeled the 100% principle.

"When I walked off the beach into our apartment, as a novice newlywed," I told Peter, "I pulled a Bible off the bookshelf and read those words from Ephesians. I'm sure they had been there all along, and I guess I'd read them—but somehow for the first time in my life it gave me a vision of something I'd never seen before. I saw myself making hard choices to serve Sherry with a 100% commitment."

I noticed Peter's eyes had a distant look—as if I were lecturing him on nuclear fission. "Are you wondering how an event that took place 2000 years ago could possibly have meaning for your marriage in the 1990s?"

He nodded. "Exactly!"

To help him get my point, I listed a sequence of contrasts between the way we normally treat our wives and the power commitment Jesus makes to us, His followers:

- "I tend to impress my wife with my strength, but she reacts against my pride."
  —Jesus laid aside His strength, and has made himself approachable.
- "I wish I could force my wife into obedience, but she rejects my manipulation."
  —Jesus forgives me for my disobedience, and wins my devotion through His devotion to me.
- "I want to demand my rights as a husband, and my wife digs in her heels."
  —Jesus laid aside His rights as God, humbled himself and is therefore winsome and attractive to me.
- "I crave my wife's respect and am offended when I don't receive it."
  —Jesus deserves my respect but forgives me when He doesn't receive it.
- "I have a limit to how much I will serve my wife."
  —Jesus' love knows no limits.
- "I operate according to give-and-take."
  —Jesus operates according to give and give and give some more.

I decided to let Peter have it with both barrels at point-blank range. "The only way you can avoid smothering and killing your wife is for you to lay down your life for her. That's what the Bible asks us to do, and that's what the 100% principle is all about. It seems totally contradictory, but the way you win your wife's affection is to lay down your life for her. When she's convinced that you're willing to do anything in the world for her, then she may become willing to do anything in the world for you.

"But you're afraid she'll take advantage of you—am I right?" Peter nodded. "Actually," I went on, "once she's convinced of your 100% commitment to her, you'll have won her trust, loyalty, support, devotion, and admiration. I can almost guarantee that your wife would never go after another man when she's fully convinced she has you."

Love Is A Choice

Peter and I stood and dusted off our pants and exchanged high-fives. I can still remember what he told me. For Peter, it was unusually sober and reflective. He admitted that he was not sure whether he was prepared to make a 100% commitment to his wife, but he said, "You're the first person to tell me this—but deep down I knew it all along."

"No kidding?" I replied.

"Yeah, you're the first guy who ever had the guts to tell it like it is. I always knew marriage was so special that it would require a higher quality love than the kind we see in the movies. I want to learn about that kind of love . . . I really do."

As he climbed into his pickup to leave, I felt inadequate to do anything substantial for Peter. Yet I earnestly wanted his marriage to work. If I could sing, I'd have pulled out my guitar and sung him a song by one of my favorite contemporary musicians, Don Francisco, entitled "Love Is Not a Feeling."

Now that we've looked at a number of ego issues that weigh us down in marriage, we'll be shifting our focus in the next section to five specific areas in which we can learn to more effectively love our wives—romantic love, priorities, sexual fulfillment, spiritual life, and domestic duties. For now, enjoy these lyrics:

LOVE IS NOT A FEELING

So you say you can't take it, the price is too high
The feelings have gone,
    It seems the river's run dry
You never imagined it could turn out so rough
You give and give and give and still
    It's never enough
Your emotions have vanished
    that once held a thrill
You wonder if love could be alive in you still
But that ring on your finger
    was put there to stay
You'll never forget the word
    you promised that day
Jesus didn't die for you because it was fun
He hung there for love because
    it had to be done
And in spite of the anguish,
    His word was fulfilled
'Cause love is not a feeling, it's an act of your will
Love is not a feeling, it's an act of your will
Now I wouldn't try to tell you
    that it's easy to stand
When Satan's throwing everything
    that's at his command
But Jesus is faithful, His promise is true
And the things that He asks,
    He gives the power to do.

Section Two

THERE IS HELP

This brief allegory dramatizes a significant marital principle. Hopefully, you can see something of yourself in it, as I have.

Our hometown Atlanta Hawks were blown away by the Detroit Pistons, but it wasn't a total loss for my family on that evening. Spud Webb scored an impressive season high of 22 points, and some of the Atlanta players stopped before hitting the locker room to sign my son's program. Then we hit the chilly streets for our drive home.

Driving out of the parking lot, we passed a sidewalk vendor peddling enormous red candy apples. I thought I'd safely avoided any requests when my ten-year-old daughter yelled from the backseat, "Aw, Dad, can we get one?" As far as I was concerned, it had already been a full—and expensive—evening. Just as I was prepared to say *no*, I caught my wife's pleading eyes. It was one of those *Aw-come-on-be-a-nice-guy* expressions.

To make my only daughter a little happier, I jumped out and made the purchase. But we had not anticipated the effect that the twenty-degree temperature would have on the candy coating. It had become impenetrable as bulletproof glass. My daughter's jaw was no match for the candy glaze, and in a few minutes her frustration was affecting all of us.

Convinced that she wasn't trying hard enough, I took the apple, opened my mouth as wide as my jaw hinge would allow, and . . . My incisors and bicuspids might as well have collided with granite. A second, third, fourth time. No success. Humiliated, I changed my strategy. I thrust out my lower jaw and banged the apple against my teeth, trying to crack the stubborn glaze, but even that approach was unsuccessful.

By now I was snorting with rage over my inability to crack the surface and get down to the meat of the apple. *I will not be defeated,* I told myself. *I will conquer this dumb little apple one way or another.*

I decided to give it one final whack. Holding the apple an arms' length from my mouth, I opened wide—curling back my lips so they would not get in the way of the impact—and in one final effort of desperation . . . *smack!* The stick snapped and the apple dropped into my lap, as solid and self-contained as before. What a painful defeat!

That night I think my family had a better time watching me assault the candy apple than they did watching the Hawks. Eventually, I did break through the hard shell. We got down to where the juices flowed, and it was delicious indeed.

This playful comedy routine is more than a slice from the real-life sitcom of the Hartley family. It's an allegory about real-life marriages.

Any marriage can look bright and shiny on the surface, but to be successful, a husband and wife must learn how to crack through the surface to develop a relationship, down where the meat of life is satisfying and the sweet juices flow.

Juices

We're all familiar with the implications of the word "juice" or "juicy." "I heard a *juicy* one" means "I learned some highly classified, fascinating information that's enough to make you drool." It's a comment that heightens our curiosity and whets our appetite for more details.

In a relationship, the juice represents the intimate, the vulnerable, the sweetest aspects of any relationship. These things keep a relationship from shriveling up, drying out, caving in. We all crave the juice of life and love the way a bee craves nectar.

If a marriage is successful, it operates down where the juices flow. Effective husbands and wives learn how to communicate with each other on an intimate level emotionally, intellectually, physically, and spiritually. They learn to share with each other their insecurities, their fantasies, their dreams, their prayers— things they have never shared with anyone else. That's what it means to have a juicy marriage.

The juice of life and love is what this section is all about.

6

"But I Still Can't Figure Her Out"

"What is the most fulfilling act in your marriage?"
Ask a group of men, and they will erupt in boisterous laughter.
Stupid question. Sexual intercourse—of course.

Ask a group a women the same question, and you'll get somewhat different answers:

"Holding each other tight."

"Sitting side by side, sipping coffee, and talking in front of the fireplace."

"Taking a walk together and sharing our dreams."

Sure, women enjoy sex. But men and women have different perspectives on romantic love and intimacy in marriage. Until a man understands the difference, his relationship will never reach its maximum potential.

> ## Fact: Most men use the words *sex* and *romantic love* interchangeably. Most women do not.

Gag Book

True story. A number of years ago a gag book was published entitled *Everything I Know About Women*. It was approximately 200 pages and was published in hardback. On the outside, it looked like a perfectly normal volume, but as you flipped to the inside you quickly got the joke: It contained nothing but blank pages. The author knew he'd connect with a vast audience of men who probably could have "written" that book themselves.

You and I can survive not understanding certain aspects of our wives' individual personalities, but if we can't understand their perception of romantic love we're in trouble.

I don't know a married man—no matter how long he's been married—who claims to have figured out his wife. We all respond to this inability differently. On the one hand, it can motivate us toward admiration, respect, or a deep sense of adventure with our spouses. On the other hand it could potentially drive us to frustration, baldness, impotency, or even in some extreme cases to mental insanity. Let's consider both options.

Why Can't a Woman . . .

When Jarvis asked to have lunch together, he whispered to me that he wanted to talk about his marriage. While we were seated at a Mexican restaurant still holding our menus, I began to understand why he'd whispered about our topic of conversation. He was confused, scared, and feeling as though he were the only guy in the world who couldn't put his finger on what was wrong.

Rather than repeating our conversation, let me summarize the symptoms he identified:

- To his knowledge, his wife had never reached orgasm in their three years of marriage.
- At times they would not utter a single word to each other for three or four days.
- They had no mutual friends.
- They could not agree on a church to attend.
- She used to cry almost every day, but had suddenly stopped eight months before—and as far as he knew she hadn't cried since.
- Their vacations were always to see family—usually hers.
- She enjoyed reading, and he enjoyed outdoor recreation.

- He'd been sleeping in the guest bedroom for the past three months.

As we sipped diet colas, Jarvis finally broke down in an outcry of desperation, "Why can't a woman be more like a man?" He sounded as if he were singing two-part harmony with Rex Harrison in *My Fair Lady*.

But this was no time for song lyrics—Jarvis was obviously unable to connect emotionally, mentally, romantically, or sexually with his wife. No wonder he was discouraged and frustrated. "I don't want a divorce," he admitted, "but at this point I have no hope. If I can't figure her out, we'll never make it."

Obviously, Jarvis had keenly discovered there is a big difference between men and women, but it left him utterly exasperated. He said he was confused and that trying to communicate to his wife was like trying to speak in a language he'd never heard before.

Over lunch I told him about a Pennsylvania coal miner who was much older and wiser than both of us.

The Coal Miner

I once was asked by a vibrant elderly couple who were preparing to celebrate their sixtieth anniversary to preside over the reaffirmation of their wedding vows in a small garden wedding. What an honor!

The husband had been a coal miner in Pennsylvania and still had a well-toned muscular body. Before he retired, his wife had made him a pie every day of his life. He would eat half at the evening meal, and would take the other half to the coal mine the next day in his lunch bucket. "His favorite is butterscotch," his wife offered with a glint in her eye. She could still make a mean pie—a skill I benefited from several times.

Their anniversary celebration was simple and very special. A small group of wonderful friends gathered near an attractive gazebo in their mobile home park. To look at them, you'd have thought they were being married at Westminster Abbey. They walked toward me arm-in-arm—he, giving us all a lesson in chivalry, and she, loving every minute of it. After the vows, I announced that it was time for him to kiss the bride. He grabbed her with a zeal uncommon among teenagers, twirled her over his outstretched knee, and spun her around on her back while in a passionate embrace. Never in my life have I seen a more prolonged kiss at a wedding! Everyone hooted and hollered and whistled. There was no sense of inappropriate behavior—when you've been married sixty years, you can get away with just about anything. After a full two minutes, he stood her upright again, and I pronounced the benediction. Quietly and without the slightest tinge of embarrassment she turned and said, "He always was a good kisser."

I walked with them back to their mobile home. They were yet arm-in-arm, and she couldn't take her eyes off him as he just strutted like a peacock in full plumage. It was then I caught what may have been the only words I heard him say all day. At least these are the only words I remembered. Shaking his head he chuckled, "And you know, I still can't figure her out."

Wow, I sighed. *Sixty years together, totally in love with each other, yet he still can't figure her out. Incredible!*

And then his bride just fluttered her eyes, swatted his big, burly chest, and stated something just as important: "But he sure does try hard!"

I felt as if I had gotten a graduate school education in marriage from a coal miner and his wife. He was fully committed to the pursuit of understanding his wife. He realized it was an impossible task, for no matter how many years they lived together, there would remain more to his wife than he could comprehend. And she knew he was committed to the endless pursuit.

These folks had learned a secret of marriage that most men never discover. My coal miner friend had learned to love the mystery of marriage. I will never forget how he reveled in the wonder of his bride's complex personality.

Differences

We can either hate the differences between ourselves and our wives or we can delight in them. Chances are, they will not disappear.

Since the differences between men and women are so obvious and since men in particular often struggle with an inability to understand why women do the things they do, it is not at all surprising that the Bible addresses this subject. In a single Bible verse, we discover two skills every married man is challenged to employ. What may be surprising is that they have everything to do with romantic love.

Husbands, in the same way *be considerate* **as you live with your wives, and** *treat them with respect* **as the weaker partner and as heirs with you of the gracious gift of life, so that nothing will hinder your prayers. 1 Peter 3:7**

Two distinct commands jump out at us.

- Be considerate.
- Be respectful.

Skill #1: Be Considerate

Every English translation or paraphrase of this portion of First Peter 3:7 is worded differently:

NIV: "Be considerate as you live with your wives."

King James Version: "Dwell with them according to knowledge."

Revised Standard Version: "Live considerately with your wives."

New American Standard: "Live with your wives in an understanding way."

The English Bible: "In living with your wives, you must recognize . . ."

The Living Bible: "Be careful of your wives."

The Jerusalem Bible: "Treat your wives with consideration."

The New English Bible: "Conduct your married life with understanding."

New Berkeley: "Live understandingly with your wives."

Phillips: "Try to understand your wives."

There are equally as many ways to express this marital advice in everyday language:

- Get to know your wife.
- Find out what makes her tick.
- Discover her insecurities.
- Learn how to make her laugh.
- Recognize what makes her cry.
- Know what makes her feel good about herself . . . and what makes her feel bad about herself.
- Learn what embarrasses her.
- Discover her disappointments.
- Identify her sources of stress.
- Understand her fears.
- Hear what she is saying . . . and what she is not saying.
- Master her hot buttons.
- Learn to read between the lines.

Nine out of ten wives who say, "My husband doesn't care about me anymore," are really saying, "My husband doesn't listen," or "My husband isn't hearing what I'm saying." The extent to which our wives know that we are trying to understand how they feel is the extent to which they feel cared for. Conversely, the extent to which our wives are convinced we don't understand is the extent to which they will not feel cared for. We will not always be able to change a situation in order to please our wives or relieve their fears. But if we listen carefully and communicate a level of emotional understanding, it will go a long way toward alleviating the alienation they feel. Often, all our wives really want to know is that we are trying to understand them.

Married men score big points when they to learn how to ask

heart questions. Heart questions are designed to move our marriage beyond the superficial into the emotional, intimate, vulnerable, and personal. This is an area of romantic love into which even most hard-driving, barrel-chested bruisers fear to tread.

I enjoy asking questions to help men think deeper about their wives:

- "Pretend your wife is sitting right here with me. How would she describe what's wrong with your marriage—and what's right with it?"
- "Where is your wife hurting?"
- "What would your wife say is the most fulfilling activity the two of you do together?"
- "What are some of your wife's fears?"

As men, we are often motivated to solve our marital problems before we fully understand them. What you can overlook is that some of the problems your wife perceives can only be solved simply by understanding her. She may need no other solution.

Couples who are currently bickering over little things—how to fold the napkins, rinsing the body hairs from the shower tub, how to prepare grilled cheese—soon discover that these dumb little items sap more strength than they deserve. Often the reason for these senseless arguments is not because a woman cares so much about the particular issue—she just wants to know that you care about her feelings and thoughts on the matter.

Secret: The extent to which we convince our wife that we care how she feels about things is the extent to which we will have a successful marriage.

It's a good idea not only to ask heart questions, and to give our undivided attention to hear the answer—it's smart to repeat the answer back for the sake of clarity. Why not say something like, "Let me make sure I understand what you are saying. . . ." Then restate what you just heard her say. Sounds basic, but it may well give you a giant step forward in communicating care to your wife. Most men have no idea how lonely their wives feel when they think their husbands don't understand. When you take the time to let her know you are listening at a deep level, it communicates romantic love.

Skill #2: Be Respectful

Skill number two—*"be respectful"*—puts into practice the knowledge we learned from practicing skill number one—*"be considerate."* Once we have gained a level of understanding of our wives, we will have the potential of giving our wives something they long for just as deeply as we do—*dignity.*

My coal miner friend didn't have the resources to keep his wife clothed in brand-name outfits. But he clothed her soul in something far better—he clothed her in dignity and honor. Even in her twilight years, she remained one of the happiest, most fulfilled women I ever met.

Heart Questions

Before I paid for our colas and taco salads at the Mexican restaurant, I gave Jarvis an assignment. "I want you to find out what disappointments your wife has had in her marriage. Write them down and then let's have lunch again. Next time, it's your treat." He smiled. We shook hands. He seemed hopeful—in fact, he seemed to suddenly enter into a whole new marital perspective. Rather than letting the differences between him and his wife drive him to frustration, Jarvis seemed eager to begin an exploration of the uncharted territory of his wife's heart.

Every husband needs to learn how to ask heart questions. Feel free to borrow a few of the ones I had written on a napkin and handed to Jarvis before we left the restaurant:

• What disappointments have you faced in our marriage?

- In the next six to twelve months, what are you facing personally or what are we as a family facing that causes you fear or anxiety?
- Who is the primary person in your life right now who makes you feel good about yourself?
- When you were in school, what did other kids tease you about that made you feel hurt? Or was there anything your family teased you about when you were growing up?
- Right now, do you have a best friend?
- In our lifestyle, what are the points of greatest stress or frustration? Is there anything I can do to relieve you?
- What convictions in your life would you be willing to die for?
- The last time you cried, what were you thinking about?
- Do I ever embarrass you? In what way?

This list is certainly not exhaustive. As you learn the skill of asking heart questions, you will be able to develop a much fuller list of questions of your own. They will become like wrenches used to adjust and maintain the carburetor of your marriage. We all need to keep our hearts humming in tune with our wives'.

Using the Skills

Three days later the phone rang. Jarvis was eager to have lunch again. He was so excited he sounded as if he'd just returned from a six-month underwater exploration with Jacques Cousteau. When we met again, he could hardly express the effect his new interest had on his wife. "She opened up and told me things about herself that I never imagined—things she'd never told anyone. It was incredible! We didn't get to bed until 2:00 A.M." Then he added with a chuckle, "But I didn't care what time it was, because for the first time in months we slept together—and it was her idea!"

Sometimes relational logjams dislodge as quickly as this one. Rarely do men learn the skill of asking "heart questions" as quickly as Jarvis. And following a period of cold alienation, wives rarely thaw out so fast. But it worked for Jarvis. I was quick to point out to him that this was only the beginning and that he needed to continue employing the skill of asking heart questions and responding with respect and genuine concern. But he was certainly on the way.

Romantic love is not communicated to our wives by an erection. It's communicated through *being considerate* and *being respectful,* and that always requires talking to your wife's heart and soul. When we are willing to embrace the feelings and thoughts inside, we reach in and draw her heart close to our own. When a wife feels understood and accepted, she will feel loved and she'll be free to show love in response.

As hard as we may try to employ these two skills in our marriages, there is often one common obstacle that often gets in our way—at least, from our wives' perspective. I am referring to your job and your attitude toward it. For most of us, unwittingly, our job can become a mistress, capturing our best emotional attention and our time.

Before you say, "No—that's not true for me," let's take a little closer look at your job. . . .

"What Do You Do for a Living?"

Every wife needs to know that she is more important than her husband's career. If we fail to convince our wife of that, it will come back to haunt us. No matter how many diamonds, pearls, new cars, or vacations we give her, it will never be enough. What she wants is not primarily the stuff—what she wants most of all is to be cherished. Yet, without question, the most common rival for a woman is her husband's career.

For some women this is a bitter rivalry. And often she feels that her only means of combat is to shoot barbed arrows at her unsuspecting husband. At odd moments, even in front of other people, she'll say things like:

- "You're married to your job."
- "What do you do there all the time?"
- "Your job is more important to you than your marriage."
- "You're a workaholic."
- "How do *you* know what the kids and I should do about _____? You're not around enough to know."
- "You come home so tired, you don't have any energy left for me or the kids."
- "Your job is your mistress."
- "You might as well put a mattress in your office. Why bother coming home?"
- "I still don't understand your job."

We *hate* to hear comments like that. After busting our buns all day long, such remarks tend to slip past our defenses and hit us below the belt. After all, when we get home we are ready to loosen the tie, kick off our shoes, and just chill out for a while. We don't expect to have to justify our hard work. But after a while our worn-out response sounds hollow: "Honey, I work hard to make money to provide a nice home and a comfortable lifestyle for you and the kids." Even though we think her statements are just not true, at times we doubt ourselves and even suspect that there might be a kernel of truth to what she is saying.

What makes this point of conflict complex is that a man's career is also linked to his own self-worth. Even if we don't like our job, so much of the way a man feels about himself is gauged according to his income, job performance, and career recognition. By instinct, we see our job as a primary area of responsibility and we therefore begin to strive for fulfillment in it.

In the face of our conscientious career efforts, when our wives say careless things which do not exactly communicate the level of gratitude and admiration we're looking for, it hurts. While we don't expect them to stand up and cheer every week as our weary body drags home with a paycheck, it's confusing when they criticize our work ethic.

How can our careers, which are supposed to be the very source of our livelihood, actually become one of the greatest sources of friction? For some couples this becomes an insurmountable obstacle.

An Elevator Ride

Two men get on the same elevator. Having exchanged initial single-word greetings, do they extend their conversation? Since they both push the fifth-floor button, one passenger asks the other the non-threatening question that men have come to expect: "And what do you do?"

In our world, men tend to cubbyhole one another according to career handles. "He is a pilot for Delta." "He's a rep for a pharmaceutical company." "He is a prof at NYU." Whatever. While we're not rigidly locked in to a caste system in our culture, we're aware of the subtle status differences between blue-collar work, the professions, and corporate hierarchy positions like middle management and executive level.

One day in particular, I was the man asking my new elevator acquaintance, "And what do you do?"

He responded to my innocent question in a way I had never heard before nor since. He looked me square in the eye and with open-faced confidence stated, "I'm a husband." After giving his answer a full second to rattle around the otherwise silent elevator, he added, "I'm a husband first, and a father of five children." I enjoyed his answer too much to ask, *Yeah, okay—but what do you do to make your money?* I found it thoroughly refreshing to meet a man who saw his highest career that of husbanding and saw his role as a provider as secondary. It was refreshing to meet a stranger on the elevator who was mature enough in who he was as a man to unashamedly claim his primary identity within his own home.

I thought, *Good night! I'd love to meet your wife. She must be a highly fulfilled woman to have such devotion from a man!* His answer motivated me to pursue his friendship. His name is Max, and he has since become one of my closest friends. From him I've learned many helpful insights into being an effective husband and a happy man.

Max and I lack most things in common. I am white-collar and he is blue-collar. I wear wing tips or tassel loafers, and he wears steel-toed work boots. My hands are lily white, and his are heavily callused and cracked. He is twenty years my senior and sees life from a slightly different perspective. But when it comes to marriage we share common goals: We both want to succeed at married life and we both want to express love to our wives in terms they can understand.

Our Higher Calling

The dilemma many of us face can be stated this way:

- Our wives want to be treated as being more important than our careers.
- Our careers require more time, effort, and mental energy than our marriages.

Therefore, some men conclude that they will never be able to give their wives what they demand because it is "unreasonable."

There is another option, however, and my friend Max found it. We can make marriage our career—that is, *our marriages can be viewed as the higher calling that actually determines our self-worth.*

Do you see the major impact of such a 180-degree change in viewpoint? Once I realize that my most important identity is found in my relationship to my spouse, rather than in my business career, I can be sure my wife will feel the dramatic difference. Once this shift in my attitude has occurred, my wife's whole attitude toward my job—and toward me—is likely to change. I have never yet met a woman who didn't want her husband to succeed at his career. Wives love to watch their husbands achieve when they are positively challenged and thriving in their work.

The real male tragedies are the men whose priorities remain upside down—men who build careers outside the home while their wives remain unimpressed.

People magazine is full of celebrities whose lives illustrate my point.

Mohammed Ali was once the world's most celebrated athlete. He could "dance like a butterfly, and sting like a bee." He could knock out any opponent who dared to step in the ring, but he was TKOed three times in marriage.

Frank Sinatra—"old blue eyes"—was the heart throb of another generation, who sold millions of recordings and was befriended by U.S. Presidents. Millions of women loved his music and swooned in front of his stage, but his first four wives walked away unimpressed.

Terry Bradshaw knew how to lead his team, the Pittsburgh Steelers, down the field, score touchdowns and win four Super Bowls. He could lead a team—but he couldn't quarterback his marriage, and it ended in divorce.

Sylvester Stallone wrote, directed, and starred in a wide range of box office blockbusters, but his marriage fell apart. He was a hit with millions of viewers, but he wasn't much of a star to his wife.

Even the celebrated sex therapists and marriage counselors Dr. Williams Masters (age 76) and Virginia Johnson (67) were divorced after twenty-one years of marriage because of "a difference in goals."

Donald Trump, who could negotiate billion-dollar deals, failed to maintain his marriage with Ivana.

The list goes on and on . . . men who learned how to make money but lost their marriages in the process—men who were successful in their careers outside their homes, but failed tragically within their homes.

The purpose of presenting this list is not to shame or discredit these men, or to heap misery on any of you who have already suffered the consequences of divorce. It is easy to see, however, that success in business does not in any way guarantee success in marriage. There may even be a subtle relationship between public success and marital failure. Perhaps men who become so tremendously popular for accomplishments outside the home tend to lose their focus on finding self-esteem inside the home. Perhaps the hearts of such men are more prone to enjoy the arena where they receive the louder applause.

As a man who is involved in a public career—pastoring, preaching, writing, and giving motivational talks—and one who is explicitly committed to maintaining the primary focus on my family—I have chosen to be particularly sensitive toward this temptation to run to the applause. Personally, I do not want to speak to enormous crowds and sell millions of books, or to pastor an ever-growing congregation, and bomb out at marriage in the process.

The choice of which career is of highest priority is a choice each man must make for himself.

Max's Wife

Listening to Max brag about his wife gave me a high level of expectation. When I met her, I was not disappointed.

She is physically attractive, but her greatest beauty seems to come from within. She has a dynamic, virtuous character that is most impressive, and her commitment to Max is rock solid. She seems as eager to please him as he is to support her. As Sherry and I got to know them better as a couple, we would frequently hear her say, "Max likes it when I . . . ," and "I think Max would want me to . . ." Their relationship has somehow avoided the syrupy infatuation or the sickening co-dependence that often characterizes unhealthy marriages. They thrive in their own individual lives, yet they mutually encourage each other.

One evening as Sherry and I were driving from their home, I commented enviously, "She sure treats him like a king."

"Yeah," Sherry agreed, "but that's because he treats her like such a queen."

All I could do was smile and nod in wonder. Inwardly I was silently making a new commitment to Sherry.

That day I adopted a life goal: I want Sherry to be the most happy, fulfilled woman I know. Even more than wanting to be treated like a king, I want her to feel like a queen. I will not be able to buy her all the cars, clothes, and luxuries I'd like to, but I am committed to clothe her in dignity, honor, and love. I will constantly find creative ways to convince her that she is cherished, and I will do what I can to help her find relief from the things that cause her friction, stress, and anxiety.

I have learned a handful of ways to communicate to Sherry that she is more important to me than my career. Hopefully, most of these, if not all, are transferable to your situation.

Five Ways to Convince Your Wife She's More Important Than Your Career

1. Allow her to reach you by phone without having to go through your secretary or without your having to call her back. Giving her this access is a simple way of saying, "Honey, you are more important than anything I do. The moment you want my attention, you become priority number one."
2. Take time out during your day to phone her, write her a note, schedule a lunch, or even periodically pay her a surprise visit. Telephoning during the work day or while on a business trip has a wonderful way of communicating to your spouse that even while immersed in your career, your mind and spirit still return home.
3. When overtime is necessary:

- Try to warn her in advance, when possible.
- Tell her and demonstrate to her that you appreciate the sacrifice she makes when you have to work longer hours, which communicates respect.
- Somehow make it up to her when the "season" is over. When it's not possible to pay her back with a special gift or a weekend vacation, perhaps an even better option might be flowers, a card, or a special meal together.

Wife vs. Career

1. Allow her to reach you by phone directly.
2. Take time out during your day to contact her.
3. Communicate with her about overtime.
4. Bring her into the decision-making process.
5. Reserve some of your strength every day for her.

---

4. Bring her into the decision-making process. This is most important in the selection of secretarial and office staff. Some men allow their wives to interview their secretaries before hiring, and give them veto power in the selection process. Other men make it their habit to consult their wives before any major decision. They do this, not simply to allow the wife to *feel* as though she's important, but many men, including some high-level executives, have learned the hard way that their wife's "intuition," even on issues they otherwise know little about, may be worth far more than a high-priced consultant.
5. Reserve some of your strength every day for your wife.

One evening on my way home from the office, I was particularly exhausted and feeling incapable of giving anything to anyone, not even to my wife. I had been driving behind a dump truck loaded with debris, and I was growing increasingly frustrated with how slowly the traffic was moving. Not able to find a break in the oncoming traffic to pull out and pass the truck, I resigned myself that my long day was just going to get longer behind this ugly, exhaust-belching vehicle. It was then that I thought, *Your spirit is just like that vehicle—loaded down and sluggish*. When the driver pulled the truck into the dirt road to dump its load, rather than hitting the accelerator and speeding home, I sensed something in me impressed me to stop, too. I hit my brakes and pulled over near the truck. As I watched that truck's hydraulic lift hoist the cargo bin, the huge load began to slide off. And to myself I said, *Okay, burdens, I lay you aside*. Strangely, it was as if my excess baggage of stress and anxiety slid off the flatbed of my spirit. The troubles didn't vanish, of course, but I did feel twenty pounds lighter.

As I drove away from the dump, I knew I had learned an important principle—no matter how hard my day, I need to leave emotional loads behind and reserve some strength for my wife.

Sometime between the moment you leave your place of employment and when you pull into your driveway, mentally back up your "dump truck" and off-load your stress so that you have something to give physically, emotionally, mentally, and spiritually to your family when you arrive home.

True, it's hard for us as men to step inside our wives, but just think about it—if you were a woman and were expected to give yourself wholeheartedly to a man, wouldn't you be more likely to do that if you knew your husband had totally given himself to you?

The Domestic Career

There is no more challenging career than husbanding. If we want to experience our full range of potential, as men, and if we want to understand the genius of all that God created us to be— then we need to explore all the vast regions of *husbanding*:

- Husbanding is often blue-collar—at times we need to clean gutters, change tires, and pick up dog poop in the backyard. But it develops hidden talent we didn't even know we had.
- Husbanding is sales—we need to maintain an ongoing pro-

gram to sell our wives on their own self-esteem and convince them of their personal dignity. And when we have sold them, we have a faithful customer—for life.

- Husbanding is middle management—we make purchases, balance a family budget, and manage our personal assets. Whether our resources amount to much or little, we can know the joy of consulting and cooperating with the master plan for all that is on loan to us from the One who is our Source.
- Husbanding is white-collar—we give counsel, moderate discussion, and make hard choices. The thrill of placing all that we know and all that we are on the line.
- Husbanding is also executive—"The buck stops here." We assume responsibility for the care and welfare of another person. Perhaps our greatest challenge is to help them care for themselves.

There is nothing as exciting as watching a man function well. When a star basketball player dances down the court, maneuvering past the defense as if they are playing in slow motion, I find it easy to applaud. When an F–16 pilot does loops in wing-tip formation, I watch in admiration and wonder. When the wood craftsman exhibits his oak cabinet, I marvel at his expertise. And when a husband effectively communicates to his one-and-only that she is special, I want to stand up and shout.

Men were made to feel the fulfillment of successfully loving a wife. And a man succeeds to the extent that he convinces his wife that she is the most important one in his life this side of eternity.

You may now unbuckle your seat belt and move about the cabin. I want you to be comfortable as we discuss how to enjoy sex more than you can imagine.

Mutual Sexual Fulfillment

Any mammal can reach orgasm; that doesn't take much. But it requires a certain degree of skill to experience consistent mutual sexual fulfillment. Any man realizes that reaching sexual self-fulfillment is only half the pleasure. What we all earnestly desire is for sex to be as satisfying for our wives as it is for us.

No one I know describes the exhilaration better than Mike Mason. Sit back and enjoy his laser show.*

> The genitals, positioned as they are, can hardly be engaged without the rest of the body following suit, and even as toes and fingers interlace, so noses, eyelids, lips, and tongues play and press against one another in an act that is visibly as well as emotionally and spiritually a passionate effort to unite. Even the simple act of kissing is powerfully symbolic of the crush of personalities as each partner pushes his features against those of the other as if to make one new face out of the two. Kissing implies losing face; it is inherently a free and wholehearted gesture of self-effacement.
>
> Much more than being a symbolic gesture, however, much more than a sign, intercourse is a seal. In an obvious way it is a literal union of sweat and spittle, excreta and se-

*Excerpts from the book *Tender Warrior* by Stu Weber; Multnomah Books, Queststar Publishers, © 1993 by Stu Weber.

creta, flecks and rubbings of all sorts of tissues. Less obviously, it is a union of cells, of genes and hormones, of neurons and corpuscles and electrons, and of less substantial bits as well: particles of personality, molecules of memory, brain bits and soul scrapings, to say nothing of whole clouds of emotion. Copulation is an activity which (uniquely in humans) comes close to being a systematic touching and stroking of every square millimeter of two bodies, and one which a man and a woman almost literally have to turn themselves inside out in order to perform. If this is not quite what actually takes place, it is at least what the lovers appear to be striving for, as each seems intent upon stripping off their very skin and wrapping it around the other. Sex is a cheek-to-cheek waltz of cells across the hormone-polished dance floor of flesh. It is almost as if every atom of one body were to be lined up against every atom in the other body in a one-to-one correspondence, and then vigorously rubbed together. And how the sparks do fly!

If you like Mason's description of lovemaking, listen to him crank it up a few notches as he hallucinates on the ramifications.

It is little wonder, with so much going on at the purely biological level, that what is meanwhile being whispered in the ear of the soul is no sweet nothing: On the contrary, it is almost everything there is, as much of one whole person, body and soul, as can possibly be squeezed into another. What happens visibly and corporeally in sex cannot help but resonate in the deepest chambers of temperament, psyche, and spirit. Inevitably what this means is that there is a total nakedness between two people: Nakedness not just of flesh, of touch, of eyes, but of feelings, of ideas, and of all the faintest stirrings of the soul. We may not think of the removal of clothes as being a revelation of our thoughts and character, but that in fact is exactly what happens. Just as the very awareness of nakedness, which is the shame of sin, renders it difficult for man effectively to hide himself from God, so the frank exposure of that nakedness in sex makes it much harder for a man and a woman to hide anything at all from each other. They may *think* they can still hide and keep secrets, but in truth they cannot, for they have become one flesh as surely as if their very nervous systems had been coupled together into the same computer network. Thereafter, what one knows, the other knows also with the deep and secret knowledge of the flesh, and they needn't kid themselves that this is not the case. Whenever anything is wrong they will both know it and will both react. When it comes to any secret, a husband may well be able to conceal from his wife *what* it is, exactly, but he can never hide the fact *that* it is. For the effects of it will already be flashing automatically through all the electronic circuits of her bone marrow. It is probable that not the slightest hint of a shadow passes across a husband's eyes that does not darken also the eyes of his wife.

And that, to state it bluntly, is what is always and inevitably involved in two people jumping into bed.

Sexual Unfulfillment

With the offer of sexual satisfaction dangled in front of our faces every day on billboards, magazines, and videos, why do so few marriages experience it? And why do so few wives consistently reach orgasm?

A man may tolerate six months or six years or even longer without a mutually satisfying sex life, but sooner or later it will have a debilitating effect. Deep down every man feels like a failure if he can't reach orgasm, and deep down when his wife doesn't reach orgasm, he feels like half a failure.

When Kurt called me, he said his marriage was drying up but he didn't know why. As he told me his story, I began to put some pieces together. Kurt had been:

- Popular in high school
- Dated around
- Sexually active in college
- Married early
- Wife became increasingly frigid
- Unfaithful to his wife
- A few scattered one-night stands with business acquaintances

"I know our marital problems are my fault," he admitted, "but

I hate to make love with a woman who doesn't respond to me. I might as well go to bed with a mannequin."

It quickly became obvious to me that Kurt was making the same classic mistake millions of other American males make. I had to call it the way I saw it.

"Kurt, the scope of your masculinity is wrapped up in your sexual organ. There's a lot more to being a man than reaching orgasm." I paused to make sure he wasn't reaching for his revolver to blow my head off. "Kurt, you know as well as I do, it's no fun just going through the motions with a woman who is not as sexually aroused as you are. But what makes that so annoying is that deep down inside, it makes us feel undesirable and impotent. And that's hard to deal with."

Even though I was hitting hard, I could see Kurt taking it all in. Without ever flinching, he looked me straight in the eye. "Okay, you're right. But what do I do about it?"

Help!

Over the next several weeks I met with Kurt a few times. We talked about five primary principles that combine to promote a mutually fulfilling sex life:

1. Start preparing days in advance for a sexually fulfilling evening.

A healthy sex life is the product of an ongoing, mutually stimulating, balanced relationship. In order for a wife to enjoy sexual intimacy, she needs to feel special, understood, relaxed, supported, and cherished. Before we intertwine sex organs, we need to intertwine our minds, emotions, and personalities. Before we get to the bedroom, we need to invest some meaningful talk-time in the living room. Men and women are wired much different at this point.

- A woman needs time to talk, unwind, feel well rested and cared for before she will be ready to make love.
- A man, on the other hand, can drag himself home dead tired, eat dinner without saying a word, fall asleep in front of the

TV, climb into bed, snore for ten minutes. Then, the moment his wife's bra straps pop and she slides between the sheets, he is suddenly salivating for fulfillment.

There's nothing wrong with the way a man is wired, and there's nothing wrong with the way a woman is wired, but if there is no heart-to-heart understanding the whole relationship will be dangerously short-circuited. Any smart man who wants to have sexual fulfillment in the evening will begin whispering it into his wife's ear at least the night before.

---

2. **The power of your sex life is determined by the purity of your sex life.**

Christians are no longer the only ones touting the virtues of purity. Even Hollywood hunk Warren Beatty was quoted in *Vanity Fair* as saying, "The highest level of sexual excitement is in a monogamous relationship."* What we need to understand is that fidelity is not simply physical—it is mental and emotional.

It angers me that some marriage counselors are still telling clients to look at pornography to jump start a stalled sex life. That is like trying to put Kool-Aid in the tank when the car is out of gas. Too many things indicate that looking at sexually explicit videos or magazines weakens your marriage.

- Our goal is not a good sex life—our goal is a good marriage. It is a fatal mistake to reverse this order. Marriage does not exist to legalize and showcase sex. Sex exists as a means of expressing love for a spouse and to promote a marital relationship.
- If a man whose wife is already having problems with intimacy encourages her to look at pornography together with him, he will only dig himself further in the hole. She will feel cheated, insecure, inferior, lonely, and abused.
- A man is ordinarily far more visually oriented than his wife.

---

*Warren Beatty, *Vanity Fair* (November 1991).

He will be more easily aroused by the pornography than his wife. He will feel the pressure for release more quickly, which will, in turn, only widen the gap in their fulfillment levels. *Backfire!*

- The husband who looks at pornography places unfair comparisons on his wife, while making her feel terribly inferior.
- A man who fantasizes about other women while having sex with his wife is engaging in mental prostitution, and he is roadblocking any real hope for his marriage.
- Sexual desires that are unrighteously aroused will never be righteously fulfilled.

If you are hooked on pornography (or even if you are just dabbling), you need help. It is not a victimless crime. You are a victim and so is your wife. (Not to mention the "models" who are being hooked into a demeaning, hellish lifestyle—supported by your money.) You are defiling the purity and potential of your own sex life. Don't blame your wife for not satisfying all your cravings. Lusts that have been unrighteously aroused, will never be righteously fulfilled. Your wife is incapable of fulfilling such cravings. It's not her problem, it's yours!

Focus on your wife. I take this very seriously, partially because I love my wife and partially because I want to have the most potent sex life possible. And I fully realize that if I waste myself physically, mentally, or emotionally on any other woman, I am wasting my potential.

- I see myself as a one-woman man. Any other woman is, in a spiritual and emotional sense, a strange woman.
- I have committed my eyes never to look twice at another woman. ("I made a covenant with my eyes not to look lustfully at a girl" (Job 31:1).
- I have memorized a number of Bible verses to help me guard my thoughts and eyes when my evil desires want to violate my commitment. (These "Resistance Verses" are at the end of this chapter.)

"Purity in the Workplace"

1. Only speak positively about your wife and your marriage in public.
2. Never listen to a woman in the workplace talk about her marital problems. Direct her to professional help and leave it there.
3. Never try to meet another woman's emotional needs.
4. Ask your wife to interview your secretary to make sure your spouse approves. Give your wife veto power.
5. Maintain a business, professional relationship at all times.
6. Always avoid physical contact. Too many working relationships have gone sour even by innocently passing paper clips hand to hand. Next time it's a back rub, then a hug, then it's too late.
7. Never ask your secretary to meet your personal or domestic needs. She should not sew a button on your shirt or take your suits to the laundry.
8. Never become emotionally involved with another woman. Never listen to detailed sexual problems. Never pray alone with the opposite sex unless she is twenty years older or younger and then only once.
9. Only counsel a married woman with her husband's permission.
10. Allow your wife to immediately get through to you by phone. At that moment she becomes the most important person in your world.

- In our offices we maintain high standards in order to achieve moral excellence in the workplace.
- I meet with a small group of men every week to hold me accountable in my personal, moral, and spiritual life. They consistently ask me six penetrating questions.

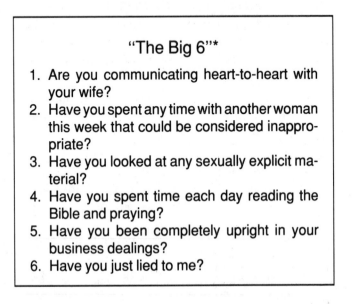

"The Big 6"*

1. Are you communicating heart-to-heart with your wife?
2. Have you spent any time with another woman this week that could be considered inappropriate?
3. Have you looked at any sexually explicit material?
4. Have you spent time each day reading the Bible and praying?
5. Have you been completely upright in your business dealings?
6. Have you just lied to me?

- In our home, my wife and I have agreed never to use the words "divorce," "separate," "leaving home," or "run away."
- We never watch a movie, TV program, or video that has a situation involving adultery, divorce, or flirtation outside of marriage, whether or not any nudity appears on the screen.
- We never allow members of the opposite sex to discuss their marital problems with us.
- I do not pray with women—not even in counseling sessions. I tell women, "After you leave my study, I'll pray for you for five minutes." And I do.

I am not nervous about these guidelines and I don't think I'm hyper—but neither am I foolish. I am warned by the proverb: "Beware when you think you stand lest you fall" (1 Corinthians

---

*Inspired by Chuck Swindoll's list of seven questions from his book *Rise and Shine*, p. 211.

10:12). As a professional Christian minister, there are enough of my colleagues who have morally bit the dust to fill a phone book. I don't want to become another statistic.

Bottom line: Sexual power comes from sexual purity because God made it that way. Sex is not a dirty word, it is a holy word. And for that reason it is to be held in highest regard. True sexual intimacy is the by-product of a loyal, trusting, purehearted, exclusive relationship between one husband and one wife who have diligently saved themselves—fighting off every other option—solely for each other.

———

3. Understand and appreciate the mysteries of your wife's anatomy, her personal chemistry, and her monthly cycle.

Some men laugh at the suggestion that they do not understand their wives' bodies. However, when I ask them to identify the clitoris, they think I'm referring to a mouthwash or foot powder. The clitoris is in some ways to the female what the penis is to the male. It is the primary female organ that responds to stimulation. Without understanding the exact position of this organ in foreplay, the husband might as well try to arouse her by fondling her bunions.

If you think you're such an expert in female physiology, let me ask you another question. "Who gets an erection, the husband or wife?" While some men think erection is distinctly male, that is not correct. Just as a man's penis fills with blood and therefore stands erect when stimulated, so does a woman's vagina—it is flared and firm and moistened when stimulated. This simple understanding helps a man understand when his wife is "ready."

While many contemporary marriage books are divided on this issue in relation to hygiene, there is good logical reason for a couple to refrain from sexual activity during the woman's monthly cycle. This allows time for the woman to expel the unfertilized seed and the accompanying blood—and it further gives the husband time to express his love for her in other nonsexual, sensitive ways. Most wives appreciate this sensitivity. After a full seven days or longer of such mutual, voluntary abstinence, resuming sexual activity can rival the honeymoon for excitement.

----

4. **Make it your primary goal to gratify your wife's sexual desires, not your own. Never demand sex.**

    We have all heard our wives repeat those disappointing words:

    - "I have a headache."
    - "I'm too tired."
    - "My period started yesterday."
    - "I'm just not up for this tonight."
    - "I'm too stressed out."
    - "I just don't feel close to you right now."

At times those words are devastating, especially when we are not feeling good about ourselves otherwise. When things are going bad at work or when the bills outweigh our pay check and we feel under the crunch, a bedtime denial can feel similar to castration. Instead of pouting, there is a much better route.

Too many husbands pout for sex. Inside, it makes them feel childish, but although they know it is demeaning, men can easily fall into this pattern out of frustration, anger, and compulsion.

It can create a revolutionary change in a marriage when the husband privately commits himself to never again demand sexual gratification, but instead commits himself to love his wife as an equal.

Make a new commitment: Never again force, manipulate, or coerce sex from your wife. Such behavior cheapens sex for both of you—and it cheapens your marriage. Creatively, sensitively, and wisely treat your wife with concern, care, and respect.

- Give her a back rub with lotion—sometimes that works wonders to relieve the headache or the stress load.
- Spend an extra thirty minutes talking through her day and yours in the living room before you get to the bedroom.
- Always be sure to touch her in some way emotionally, romantically, before you expect to touch her physically, sexually. Ask heart questions.

- Yes, the physical need is important and it can't be ignored. As a last resort, gently suggest, "How about tomorrow night?" You will soon discover that sex twenty-four hours later with a wife who is willing, eager, and ready is far more fulfilling than with a wife who just wants to get it over with.

---

5. Keep the flame alive.

It doesn't matter if we've been married twenty, forty, or sixty years, our sexual experience in marriage can still be new, creative, and exhilarating. There are always new postures and positions, new tender words to express, new sequence, and new environment.

The most effective way to "affair-proof" your marriage is to include everything in your marriage that could potentially entice you to look elsewhere. The four most common reasons for husbands and wives to fall into an adulterous relationship are quite logical.

1. Ego needs. "She makes me feel like I'm worth something."
2. Romance. "He treats me special."
3. Companionship. "I was so lonely."
4. Sex. "I was just horny."

This may or may not be obvious, but the large majority of adulterous relationships are not initiated because of a desire to have sex. In fact, that is the least common reason. A man's most common motivation is ego needs. A woman's most common motivation is romance. A key to any marriage is, to be sure, meeting each other's needs for self-worth and romance.

A few specific ideas:

- Periodically, spend the money on a weekend alone. It's a lot cheaper than marriage counseling.
- Every Christmas, birthday, Mother's Day, or Valentine's Day, add something beautiful to your wife's undergarment drawers.
- At least once a year, take your wife to a fine restaurant as a date for the expressed purpose of discussing mutual sexual fulfillment—what works and what doesn't work, what does she

find pleasing and what is a turnoff? You may not hear what you wanted to hear and you may even need to listen between the lines. But if you are willing, she could give you graduate school training in how to satisfy her sexually.

Our problem is, many men are not willing. Many men are so sexually pumped up through undisciplined thought lives that all they want is what they want, when they want it, the way they want it. Such a ballistic, out-of-control sex drive will never be fulfilled. Period. No matter who the sex partner is. Men who are so sexually willful are themselves not willing to learn to meet the needs of their spouses. Such an attitude brutally defies the potential of a mutually potent sex life.

Intimacy

When Kurt had listened to my monologue on mutual sexual fulfillment, he volunteered, "Some of what you told me I already knew. I should have known most of it, but quite honestly, I didn't. But I must admit, no one—not my father, not my college buddies, not my wife—ever laid it out there like you just did. Thanks."

Then he added something that was good to hear: "The thing that came through most clearly is the new mind-set I need. Sex is not something to simply gratify my male instincts; it is to be gratifying to both of us. That makes sense."

When the phone rang six months later, at first I didn't recognize Kurt's voice when he asked for an appointment. When he sat in my study his countenance confirmed the good news he came to tell me.

"I feel like a new man," Kurt began. "Our marriage is brand new."

He went on to tell me something he had withheld from me before. He had been involved with another woman when he visited the first time. No wonder Kurt struggled with insensitivity toward his wife. Now that other relationship was ended and mutual trust was being restored.

"I fully respect my wife's romantic needs," Kurt confessed, "and I'm committed to never again violate her conscience."

No question about it—the flame of his love was alive, and he was savoring the benefits of living within the parameters of holy marriage.

Sex is great. We can imagine all kinds of sexual fulfillment—but no mental peep shows aimed at your own selfish fulfillment will ever compare to mutual sexual fulfillment.

And now I have news for you that may be difficult to believe: While sex is great, it is not *the* greatest. In this next chapter we will investigate something that is . . . well, better than sex.

Resistance Verses

Luke 11:4b—"Lead us not into temptation, but deliver us from the evil one."

Exodus 20:17—"You shall not covet your neighbor's house. You shall not covet your neighbor's wife, or his manservant or maidservant, his ox or donkey, or anything that belongs to your neighbor."

Job 31:1—"I made a covenant with my eyes not to look lustfully at a girl."

Psalm 101:2b–3a—"I will walk in my house with blameless heart. I will set before my eyes no vile thing."

Psalm 119:9—"How can a young man keep his way pure? By living according to your word. . . I have hidden your word in my heart that I might not sin against you."

Matthew 5:8—"Blessed are the pure in heart, for they will see God."

Matthew 5:27–29—"You have heard that it was said, 'Do not commit adultery.' But I tell you that anyone who looks at a woman lustfully has already committed adultery with her in his heart. If your right eye causes you to sin, gouge it out and throw it away. It is better for you to lose one part of your body than for your whole body to be thrown into hell."

Matthew 6:22–23—"The eye is the lamp of the body. If your eyes are good, your whole body will be full of light. But if your eyes are bad, your whole body will be full of darkness. If then the light within you is darkness, how great is that darkness!"

Romans 6:11–14—"In the same way, count yourselves dead to sin but alive to God in Christ Jesus. Therefore do not let sin reign in your mortal body so that you obey its evil desires. Do not offer the parts of your body to sin, as instruments of wickedness, but rather offer yourselves to God, as those who have been brought from death to life; and offer the parts of your body to him as instruments of righteousness. For sin shall not be your master, because you are not under law, but under grace."

Romans 8:12–14—"Therefore, brothers, we have an obligation—but it is not to the sinful nature, to live according to it. For if you live according to the sinful nature, you will die; but if by the Spirit you put to death the misdeeds of the body, you will live, because those who are led by the Spirit of God are sons of God."

2 Timothy 2:19–22—"Nevertheless, God's solid foundation stands firm, sealed with this inscription: 'The Lord knows those who are his,' and, 'Everyone who confesses the name of the Lord must turn away from wickedness.' In a large house there are articles not only of gold and silver, but also of wood and clay; some are for noble purposes and some for ignoble. If a man cleanses himself from the latter, he will be an instrument for noble purposes, made holy, useful to the Master and prepared to do any good work. Flee the evil desires of youth, and pursue righteousness, faith, love and peace, along with those who call on the Lord out of a pure heart."

1 John 2:14b–17—"I write to you, young men, because you are strong, and the word of God lives in you, and you have overcome the evil one. Do not love the world or anything in the world. If anyone loves the world, the love of the Father is not in him. For everything in the world—the cravings of sinful man, the lust of his eyes and the boasting of what he has and does—comes not from the Father but from the world. The world and its desires pass away, but the man who does the will of God lives forever."

Jude 1:24–25—"To him who is able to keep you from falling and to present you before his glorious presence without fault and with great joy—to the only God our Savior be glory, majesty, power and authority, through Jesus Christ our Lord, before all ages, now and forevermore! Amen."

Revelation 1:5b–6—"To him who loves us and has freed us from our sins by his blood, and has made us to be a kingdom and priests to serve his God and Father—to him be glory and power for ever and ever! Amen."

Revelations 18:4—"Then I heard another voice from heaven say: 'Come out of her, my people, so that you will not share in her sins, so that you will not receive any of her plagues.' "

Better Than Sex

Just as the hymen is ruptured in initial intercourse, marriage demands the tearing of previously unpunctured emotional and spiritual membranes in the pursuit of intimacy. This is often a painful and even visceral process. Deep within us all are emotional and spiritual realms that are highly personal. And they are begging to be explored.

Sexual intercourse has been described in many ways—stimulating, exhilarating, energizing, spine-tingling, titillating, captivating, even euphoric. It may be one experience that defies accurate description. However, despite popular opinion to the contrary, sex is not the ultimate aspect of marriage. And, believe it or not, it is potentially not even the most fulfilling. It does get better than sex. (To a sex-saturated society this may be a hard sell, but I'm willing to try.)

Deeper Than Orgasm

Prior to marriage I wrestled with the hypothetical possibility of my wife someday being injured, scarred, in some way afflicted with a debilitative disease, or physically handicapped. I asked myself, *Would my love and my commitment to her survive?*

I needed the assurance, prior to walking the aisle and reciting my vows, that I had a deeper dimension to my love than the physical attraction. *What if her pretty face was no longer a pretty face—would my loyalty and faithfulness remain intact? And, God forbid, what if an automobile accident or some other unforeseen disaster would strip her of her physical abilities? Was I prepared to carry on a love affair that could potentially become a one-way street?*

These questions became more than just idle, late-night conversation with my college roommate. I was demanding answers because I sincerely needed to discover that the marriage covenant was in fact made out of an indestructible fabric. I reasoned, *If orgasm is the depth of the wedding covenant and if it does not get any deeper, higher, stronger than that, then marriage is held together only by a thin thread.* Because sexual union is utterly contingent on two reasonably healthy bodies that may or may not continue to function properly.

The Plague

Months before our engagement, Sherry flew to Florida to spend a long weekend with my family, while I was still probing the depths of the marriage covenant—without satisfactory resolution. When Sherry stepped onto the beach in her bathing suit, however, she learned—too late—that her Michigan skin was no match for the unrelenting Florida sun. Quickly, she was stricken with a most bizarre variety of sun poisoning. Instead of the usual pink rash, she was covered with random black dots that stuck out of her skin like raisins. She had a big black lump on her lip, her eyelid, and dozens of others scattered over her chin, cheeks, forehead, and neck. Her appearance was so distorted, I honestly think I could have walked right past her on the sidewalk and not known who she was. Or I might have even looked in the other direction to avoid nausea. It was nasty!

In less than a single afternoon my beautiful girl friend had lost her good looks. Now it was more than an intellectual exercise—I had a real chance to plug my speculations into life. *Isn't this precisely what you've been looking for? You want to discern whether or not your love for Sherry is merely skin deep. What more could you want?*

Now those hypothetical questions I had discussed with my college roommate entered the immediate and the practical. The

harder I probed the more I understood that, ultimately, what attracted me to Sherry was not the physical nor the sensual. It was more than her tanned skin, her clear eyes, her radiant face, her firm, well-toned body. As I spent time with Sherry while she suffered from the sun-poisoning plague, the more I realized I loved something about her that was deeper than her physical beauty. The aspect I loved most about Sherry was her spirit.

I discovered that my spirit loved Sherry's spirit. I had yet to ask her father and mother for permission and we had yet to work out the details, but in my mind the matter had been settled. I realized we would someday be married. I had answered the ultimate question: *If I marry her, what will hold our marriage together?* Bottom line: *The union of our spirits.*

At the time, Sherry was feeling so terrible about her plague and the effect it had on her physical appearance. She was convinced I was turned off. Little did she realize that the sickness was having precisely the opposite effect. It was the very thing that convinced me I could move forward. To this day we playfully talk about "the plague."

In a sense, "the plague" ripped off both our masks. It took our relationship past the superficial. We had to move deeper than:

- "Wow, aren't we a sharp-looking couple?"
- "Don't we look great together?"
- "I'm physically attracted to your outward beauty."

It took our relationship into the union of personalities.

Your Plague

I have often thought that I was fortunate to face "the plague" before marriage—to consciously realize, before we were even engaged in sexual intercourse, that sex would not be the ultimate, that there was more powerful glue holding us together. Most couples don't come to this realization—if they ever do—until they are in marriage.

Let me ask you, has your marriage faced "a plague"? Plagues come in various forms, but they always test a marital infrastructure:

- A prolonged illness
- A financial crisis
- Caring for a parent
- A career change
- A strong-willed child or a rebellious teenager

Plagues are crises we would never choose, obstacles we cannot orchestrate. They have a way of crawling up in our laps, getting in our faces and ripping our masks off. They also have the potential of taking our relationships deeper by removing some of our superficial distractions. If we do not respond to them aright, though, they have the potential to destroy us.

By the time Troy and Brenda moved in next door, their marriage was already on life support. For Troy, the move to Atlanta was a last-ditch effort—but Brenda was already convinced it was a lost cause. Troy had been without work for eight months since his back injury. They'd been living in a two-bedroom apartment that barely gave their four-member family enough room to turn around. Brenda's tubal pregnancy slapped a *whopping* medical bill on top of their bare-bones budget. The insurance settlement bought their new home, but the financial resource was quickly disappearing. They both agreed their relationship had begun with genuine love for each other, but now their three-year-old marriage was almost out of gas.

As we talked with one another in our living room, it became obvious that they were actually not running out of love—they were just running low on healthy perspective.

"I realize you're facing some heavy-duty problems," I ventured, "but I want to ask both of you—what qualities have you noticed in each other as you deal with these crises that you admire? Brenda, you tell Troy first." I asked Brenda first for two reasons: She was more discouraged than Troy and, being a woman, she might be better able to verbalize her feelings.

She sat in silence for a moment, looking over at me as if to say, *I never thought of it this way before.* When she spoke, it was worth waiting for. She spoke about "patience . . . tenderness . . . steadfastness . . . endurance . . . diligence . . . perseverance . . . uprightness . . . conscientiousness . . . being tough-minded." From the look on Troy's face, these were words of praise from his wife he never dreamed of hearing.

Then I asked Troy to tell Brenda what he admired about the way she was responding to their hardship. He had a little more difficulty getting the words out, but eventually he spoke about her "forgiveness, support, loyalty, diligence, faithfulness, *stick-to-itiveness,* and devotion."

Then Brenda made a statement that seemed to fly to Troy's heart like an arrow: "All I ever really wanted was a husband who loved me and cared for me and wanted children to raise." A profound revelation, too, I thought.

Troy was deeply moved. His whole approach changed, his attitude softened. "When things went bad, all I would focus on was what we were losing. I felt so bad I couldn't give you everything I wanted."

At this point Brenda's heart softened as well. She slid over next to him on the couch, put her arm around him, and said, "I already *have* everything I need for my happiness."

Troy and Brenda not only became outstanding neighbors, they have also become outstanding role models for Sherry and me, because they have allowed their "plague" to take them past the surface and develop a rich relationship . . . down where the juices of real life flow.

Bosom Friends

Now that you've read more than half the book and we've spent a few hours together, let me step into your comfort zone and ask you for some highly classified information:

- Are you friends with your wife? I mean best friends? (Don't answer quickly. Think about it.)
- Can you tell her everything? Do you?
- Do you feel secure enough in your marriage to be vulnerable? To tell her when you're afraid? When you're insecure? When you feel like a loser?

Or on the other hand:

- Are there secret closets in your life your wife knows nothing about?
- Do you ever feel lonely? Like there are things going on deep inside that your wife just doesn't understand?
- Do you sometimes shrink back and hide your real feelings from your wife? Afraid to drop your guard? Afraid you will look weak, or feel exposed?

Let me be blunt. The extent to which you are able to open up your private world to your wife is the extent to which your marriage will flourish. As much as we want to live down where the juices flow, too many of us continue to work hard to protect our surface of red candy coating. It's one thing for us to gain a level of security that allows us to ask our wives heart questions—but it's a deeper step when we allow our wives that right of entrance into our inner secret closets.

Vulnerability

During our first year of marriage, Sherry was in the thick of one of her daily crying sessions. I was trying to be a good boy. I told myself, *Keep your distance, give her space, act compassionate*—even though I was annoyed—*and pray for her.* On this particular occasion her face was buried in the pillow with such intensity it appeared as though she might be attempting suicide by suffocation. In typical fashion I asked condescendingly, "Is there anything I can do for you? I want to meet your needs."

Those words were like gasoline on an open fire. She erupted! Loud wailing was followed by the outburst, "Why don't you ever let me meet any of *your* needs?" Then she flopped back down on the mattress and stared up blankly at the ceiling.

With a single *whack,* her indictment hit the chisel with a sledge hammer and split the hardwood of my heart wide open. I proceeded to flop limply onto the mattress next to her, and we both stared up at the ceiling, motionless for a long time before I broke the silence. "You're right. You are absolutely right. I am always asking what I can do to meet your needs. But I rarely ask you to help me with my insecurities or problems. I admit, this is hard for me."

This was one of those electric moments in our marriage that opened up an area of my life I'd previously kept under the lock and key of my destructive pride.

The area was called my *heart*. If anyone had asked whether or not I shared my heart with Sherry, I would easily have said *yes*. But I would rarely talk about my weaknesses—only my strengths. In fact, I found it easier to talk with my buddies about my needs and ask them for counsel than to approach Sherry.

When we get married we realize—sometimes with a sense of alarm—that our wives will come to know us well. Few of us were ever prepared for the level of intimacy marriage actually demands. It is a frightening enough prospect to plunge into the uncharted waters of your wife's personality—and even more intimidating when your wife plunges beneath the surface in your life.

Swimming With Sharks

I'm reminded of the story about the wealthy Texan who built a reputation for himself by throwing extravagant summer parties. One year he filled his Olympic-sized swimming pool with sharks and alligators. Gathering all the guests on one side of the pool, he announced, "For the first brave person to swim across, I will give any one of these three gifts—a brand-new home in the mountains, a trip around the world, or the automobile of your choice." Everyone gasped in delight at the offer of such extravagant gifts when suddenly there was a loud *splash* . . . followed by the sound of thrashing across the surface of the pool . . . then *pop!* . . . a young man jumped out on the other side. Everyone cheered, not only at the Olympic-gold-medal-speed with which he swam but also at his bravery. The wealthy host was amazed, and confirmed that he would indeed honor his promise. He asked, "Which of the three gifts do you want, son?" The young man replied, "Right now I don't care about the gift—all I want to know is who was the idiot who pushed me?"

At times, a married man feels as though he's been pushed into an environment he is ill equipped to deal with. Getting beneath the surface with our wives and allowing them to get beneath the surface with us does feel like being thrown to the sharks. *Breathe easy!* No one is about to push you into the shark-infested waters of your wife's emotional life. And no one will force you, against your better judgment, to expose what's beneath the surface of your life. But let me dispel some fears: Despite popular opinion, most women are not carnivorous. To the contrary, once you allow your wife to get beneath the surface, you will wonder why you waited so long.

Unity

The only marriage counsel that has survived some 6,000 years is worth listening to—the only marriage advice given to the original husband and wife, Adam and Eve:

> For this reason,
> a man shall leave his father and mother,
> shall cleave to his wife,
> and the two shall become one flesh. Genesis 2:24

The words "leave," "cleave," and "become one flesh" highlight the deep unity Adam and Eve evidently felt when they declared:

> Finally, you are bone of my bone
> and flesh of my flesh. Genesis 2:23

The wonderful mystery of marriage is that ever since Adam and Eve, married couples have had the potential to discover the same depth of unity.

This unity is illustrated in the following diagram, which shows how the strength and weaknesses of a couple off-set each other.

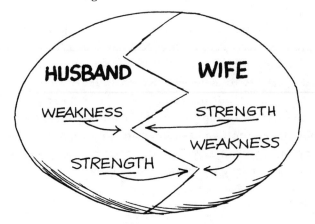

The next diagram illustrates the place at which most relationships begin—strength-to-strength.

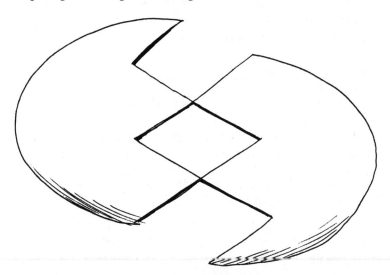

Let's say that a young man is attracted to a woman's looks, her personality, her ability. The young woman is mutually attracted because he is handsome, well-humored, kind, considerate. This point of positive attraction is where relationships begin. But if they never get past this point, the relationship will only be shallow and extremely fragile. While strengths will always be assets to marriage, a relationship that never gets beyond strength-to-strength attraction will never mature. As the diagram demonstrates, strengths will keep each other at arms' length. Such a relationship rarely lasts. It can't last. As the diagram illustrates, it has nothing to hold itself together. True intimacy is only achieved when spouses allow each other to begin to touch each other strength-to-weakness.

This third diagram shows how most marriages begin to break into intimacy and unity.

True, intimacy does not happen all at once. It is at first vulnerable, intimidating, and painful. Telling our wives our fears, insecurities, areas of inferiority and inadequacy is bad enough—but when they demonstrate strengths in our weak areas, it can become more tender and sensitive than our normal comfort level will tolerate. At times, we will recoil and jump back to what feels like a safer posture, trying to match strength-to-strength. But as the relationship matures, we will need to risk more vulnerability, because the real excitement is down where the juices flow.

The Challenge

It takes guts to unbuckle our belts and expose the underbelly hairs of our lives to our wives.

- "What if she doesn't like what she sees?"
- "What if she rejects me?"

- "What if she teases me?"

Sure, it takes guts to be a man. Anybody can keep his emotions in check, hiding his true feelings from his wife. But it takes courage and a high level of inner strength and dignity to risk our privacy for the sake of a stronger marriage.

Self-disclosure

Many times since that afternoon during our first year of marriage, I've heard the echo of Sherry's tearful plea: *"Why don't you ever let me meet any of your needs?"* Rather than waiting until she asks again, I've voluntarily humbled myself and shared with her areas of personal insecurity and weakness. It doesn't seem to get any easier over the years, but I can say with certainty that it's always worth the risk. Exposing even the dark areas of my inner life to my wife is part of my commitment to marriage. It brings me in touch with Sherry's deep love for me, and it allows her the chance to see me for who I really am.

My Neighbor and a 3×5 Card

When Troy and Brenda realized their move to Atlanta was not the quick fix their comatose marriage needed, they went to work on the real illness. They learned to communicate weakness-to-strength, and their marriage quickly came back to life. Troy shared with me an exciting idea I have found helpful. He fixed his wife dinner—just the two of them—and then asked the big conversation primer of the evening: "What disappointments have you had in our marriage?" He had no idea what to expect, but he assumed it would be high voltage. He even gave her a 3×5 card to write her thoughts down.

As Troy explained, "It was the greatest thing I've ever done." That day he learned his wife was frustrated by his lack of initiative in their personal finances. She gave him a number of practical suggestions which he has since employed. It became very obvious his weakness was an area of her strength. He also learned that she had been equally disappointed with her sex life. Just hearing her express interest gave him hope that she was in fact not a dead fish.

"My wife is now my best friend," Troy squealed with enthusiasm. "I used to have this lonely guy crawling around inside, but now she knows everything about me—and she accepts me and loves me."

Loneliness is the feeling we experience inside when there are significant areas of our lives that no one else knows about, and that no one understands. Marriage is designed to cure loneliness, but it does not cure loneliness *automatically*. The extent to which we hide significant areas of our lives from our wives is the extent to which we will continue to be lonely and alienated from them. But the extent to which we risk exposing even our weaknesses to our wives—telling them things about ourselves we've never told anyone else—that is the extent to which we'll tap into deep marital, spiritual unity.

We'll meet someone at last, spirit-to-spirit—and where intimate friendship flourishes, loneliness becomes a thing from the past.

Leadership

There is a reason why husbands need to take the initiative in this process of building intimacy—it is a matter of leadership. Many wives are waiting for their husbands to take the first step and break through the outer shell. If we intend to legitimately lead our wives and assume responsibility for our marriages and their general well-being, then we must offer leadership. Finding our dignity in marriage does not depend on keeping up false fronts that will eventually crack under their own weight—it depends on our success at leading the way to intimacy and emotional safety.

Hand your wife a 3×5 card and say, "Honey, you and I both know that I am not a perfect husband. Write on this card a couple areas in my life where you've noticed room for improvement." Husbands who have done this have come back to tell me about some great results:

- "My wife wrote down two things she'd never told me before."
- "My wife didn't dare write anything. She was afraid I'd hand her a list—but we had the best talk we've had in years."
- "My wife took the assignment seriously. She filled both sides! At first I was afraid to begin reading, but as it turned out she filled the card with things she already respects about me."
- "At first I was scared to death to try it. Finally, when I humbled myself and did it, she only wrote one word—'communication!' Then she broke down in tears and kept thanking me because she suddenly realized communication was already beginning to take place."

Warning: When you ask your wife to write down complaints and constructive criticism never hand her a legal pad. She just might fill it!

If our goal is unity and harmony, we must allow ourselves that opportunity to relate to each other strength-to-weakness and even weakness-to-weakness. Our inner wholeness depends upon it.

We have one final area of our marriage yet to investigate. And I'll give you fair warning: It is an area into which a lot of men fear to tread.

True Intimacy

The fastest way to get a room full of aggressive, loud-talking, wheeling-dealing men to become absolutely silent is to use the three little words: *"Let us pray."* Perhaps the only relationship that is potentially more intimidating than the one between a man and his wife is the relationship between a man and his God. Some of us try to quarantine ourselves against letting religion "take over" our whole lives. And some of us have been rather successful at avoiding people who want to talk seriously about God.

But then something goes wrong—terribly wrong. Our wife "gets religion" and we feel trapped.

We thought the words "let us pray" were intimidating. Then out of nowhere our wife dares to ask, "Honey, can we pray together?" We'd sooner hear her ask, "Can my mother stay with us for a month?"

Perhaps you are wondering: *How did we slip from husbands and wives making love, to husbands and wives praying together? Why do I need to read about spiritual stuff?* You may even be considering jumping to the next chapter. Hold the bus. Give me one chance to tell you about my own struggle in this area.

Do I Have To?

For the first ten years of our marriage, Sherry would periodically make the dreaded request, "Honey, could we start praying together?" Fortunately she was usually gracious and kind in the way she asked—but she was persistent. She'd been raised in a family where her parents prayed together on a regular basis. In fact, her mother wore holes in the carpet where she would kneel next to her bed to talk with God. The best I could do was to say a little prayer before meals. Pretty shabby in comparison.

Inside I was full of excuses. *Do I have to?* I thought. *After all, deep down I would rather do anything before resorting to prayer.*

I have talked with countless men on this issue who approached praying from a wide variety of perspectives. I have compiled a list of familiar reasons why it cuts across the grain to pray, particularly to pray with our wives. I know these "reasons" well: I have even used a few myself.

- "Prayer is a sign of weakness—I can do it myself."
- "Religion is a sissy thing—for women and children. Real men don't cry, and real men don't pray."
- "It is not practical. As a man I want to be involved in something I can see and touch."
- "Them that *can,* do. Them that *can't,* pray."
- "It's too touchy-feely. That's fine for my wife, because she's more emotional."
- "It doesn't come naturally. I always have to pump it up. I feel as if I'm just saying the words."
- "My faith is a very personal thing. I pray, but I pray silently. I don't have to pray out loud."
- "My wife is a powerful pray-er. She can pray for an hour. I could never compete with her."
- "It makes me feel like a hypocrite."
- "Who am I to presume that I can talk with some Supreme Being?"
- "Truthfully, the whole idea makes my skin crawl. I refuse to let my wife talk me into this one."

Can you identify?

Toward a Relationship

Why a chapter on this spiritual stuff? you ask. *What does this have to do with a successful marriage?*

The reason we dare to approach such a potentially explosive issue is that we are talking about intimacy and vulnerability—living a life that flows out of our depths. And believe it or not, there is no better way for a man and his wife to share themselves with *nothing-held-back* honesty than to do so in the presence of God. And there is no better way to touch hearts and maintain a deep level of confidentiality than through the habit of consistent prayer in marriage.

Let's face it—

- If you do not have a personal relationship with Jesus, having a consistent daily prayer time is obnoxiously unthinkable.
- But if you *do* have a personal relationship with Jesus, then *not* having a consistent daily prayer time is equally unthinkable.

For some men, having a personal relationship with Jesus seems outside the realm of possibility. *It's just not for me.* If that describes your perspective, I have news: Left to ourselves, no one could ever have a personal relationship with Jesus. Not Billy Graham. Not the Pope. Nobody. Left to ourselves, none of us have the ability to initiate a relationship with Jesus.

The good news is that we are not left to ourselves. God is no respecter of persons. He gives no special merit badges to those who attend church every Sunday, and He gives no demerits to those who go sailing instead. He loves us, not because of who we are but in spite of it. He knows us better than anyone else on earth—including our spouses—and He loves us anyway. He expressed His love for us by sending His Son, Jesus, into our perverted world.

Deep down underneath all our smoke and flimsy arguments—as much as we may hate to admit it—every man needs a relationship with God. Most of us recognize our need.

- We need an absolute value system so we can judge between right and wrong.
- We need purpose and meaning in life.
- We need a sense of inner peace and fulfillment.
- We need a cause to live for that is bigger than we are.
- We need to know for certain that when we die, we'll go to heaven.

What may come as the biggest shocker is that a personal relationship with Jesus is available to any one of us—and it can start today.

To suggest that you need to have a relationship with God in order to somehow benefit your marriage would be to sell God short. God does not exist to simply make a good marriage "a little better." He is not an aerosol can we put in the trunk of our lives in case we get a blowout. God, by definition, is Almighty, the Creator of all things. He is not just a missing piece we somehow fit into our marriage plan: Instead, our marriage is to be structured according to His plans.

Prayer is simple. It's just talking with God. We don't need to feel intimidated—He knows everything we think, but He wants us to express it in our words anyway.

The Bible quotes Jesus as giving an open invitation to all of us. "Here I am! I stand at the door and knock. If anyone hears my voice and opens the door, I will come in and eat with him and he with me" (Revelation 3:20).

If you feel a bit unstable in your relationship with Jesus, you can respond right now. Even if you have opened your heart to Him before, read this prayer carefully:

Jesus, I need you.
Thanks for loving me and for dying on the cross to show the power and depth of your love for me.
I'm so glad you rose from the dead. It's great to know you are alive.
Come into my life and cleanse me inside.
Be my Lord. Call the shots. I will put you first.
As your child I want to grow up and be obedient to you.
Thank you for giving me eternal life. And thank you for being patient with me.

If that prayer represents an inner longing, go back and read it again. Make it *your own personal* prayer.

If you are not ready to enter into that intimate relationship with God, He does not want to force you into a premature decision. Jesus is not a hard sell. He is patient and will continue to make things clearer to you.

If, on the other hand, you did sincerely pray that prayer—congratulations! A new life has begun. You will want to pay attention to the changes that will begin to take place in your life and in your marriage as Jesus takes charge. He will become as real to you as a best friend, and He will help you become a more authentic person.

Benefits of Praying Together

I know dozens of men living all over the country who have committed themselves to pray every day with their wives—just the two of them. They have shared with me some of the benefits they have received. I list them here just so your mouth can water and your heart can get motivated.

- "At first I dreaded the idea, I thought it would come back to haunt me—like my wife would use it against me. Since I've committed myself to do it, the opposite has been true—my wife respects my judgment so much more. We have a higher level of mutual trust because we are accountable—not only toward each other but toward God."

  —Marshall (Morristown, New Jersey)

- "I have always tried to live by the principle *Don't let the sun go down on your anger.* But I never really found it possible. There were always times I'd mess up, and that caused real problems in our marriage. Then when I committed myself to pray with Susan every night, it solved the problem. There is no way we can pray together when we are mad."

  —Craig (Dallas, Texas)

- "We don't pray long. But just the habit of praying every night has done so much to bind us together."

  —Jeffrey (Salem, Oregon)

- "Praying together consistently has been a real attitude check for my wife and me. It does more to weed out the negative attitudes in our home than anything."

  —Peter (Atlanta, Georgia)

- Praying together has taken our relationship into a new dimension. I always thought we had a great marriage, but now it's better than ever. We don't need to hide anything anymore. It's exciting."

—Stewart (Columbus, Ohio)

Will You Forgive Me?

After nine and a half years of marriage, I can't explain what happened, but the desire to pray consistently with my wife finally grabbed me. I knew my motives were sincere and I sensed that I had whatever it would require to consistently follow through with my commitment.

I waited until Sherry and I were all alone in the evening. I looked straight into her big brown Basset-hound eyes. "I have been neglecting my spiritual leadership in our marriage," I confessed. "I have not been initiating prayer between the two of us. Will you forgive me?"

Without any idea where I was headed, she cautiously spoke the words I was waiting to hear. "Yes, I forgive you."

"I commit myself to pray with you every night," I pledged. "And if I ever forget, I give you permission to remind me about it—just be kind." She chuckled, with tears in her eyes.

That night we hugged. We prayed. I knew Sherry was surprised—shocked might be a better word. And I sensed immediately that I had driven a significant stake that would have a permanent effect on our marriage from that night on.

That was eleven and a half years ago, and to my knowledge we have missed praying only on two nights, and they were within the first couple of months of our new commitment. On both occasions, I called Sherry the next morning, confessed my neglect, asked her to forgive me, and then briefly prayed with her over the phone. Even when I am out of town, I call home every night and we pray a la AT&T.

When we pray together there is no elaborate superstructure. We don't pray for all the missionaries of the world, nor have we seen the dead raised. Some nights it's extremely brief. When we are both dead tired it may be as brief as, "Good-night, God"— *zzzzzzzzzzzzz!* But we make contact. We touch hearts with each other, and we know for certain that no matter what we're facing in our marriage, we're not alone.

I have often reflected on the last phrase of this Bible verse:

> Husbands, in the same way be considerate as you live with
> your wives, and treat them with respect as the weaker partner
> and as heirs with you of the gracious gift of life, so that noth-
> ing will hinder your prayers. (1 Peter 3:7)

Notice, it does not say, *so nothing will hinder your sex life*, or *so nothing will hinder your communication skills*, or *so nothing will hinder your parenting*. It says, "So nothing will hinder your prayers." It has been exciting to discover why prayer is such a priority in marriage.

The Starting Point

Bringing God into our discussion on marriage should certainly not be inconceivable. It is not as if He is some kind of stranger to marriage. And bringing prayer into the marriage discussion is certainly not inconsistent with legitimate intimacy and open-hearted communications.

A few practical suggestions:

- Start by making a commitment to your wife, "Honey, I will start to lead us in prayer. Promise."
- Start small. Pray briefly. God is not impressed by verbosity.
- Alternate pray-ers: One night you pray, the next night ask your wife to pray.
- If you miss, don't worry about it. Even consistent inconsistency in prayer is better than no prayer at all.
- Don't fake it. Stay away from "professional prayers" with big words or *thees* and *thous*. Just talk English.
- Pray in faith. Jesus promises that He is right there with you when you pray in His name. Bank on it! Without faith, prayer is useless. You might as well watch TV.
- If you are too angry to pray, admit it. Go into separate rooms for five minutes. Then get back together and pray. No explanations are necessary.

We are now prepared to enter into our final section—There Is Dignity. This is where a marriage starts experiencing the benefits of playing by the rules.

Section Three

THERE IS DIGNITY

A good friend of mine recently returned from a business trip around the world without his wife. He described to me a majestic moment that seems to capture what we mean by dignity in marriage. Listen as he describes his experience.

"The place was Cape Town, South Africa—the prettiest city I have ever seen, seated on the tip of the African continent. I drove to the mountainous coastline and climbed a steep cliff with sheer rock face on either side. When I reached the top and turned around, I felt as though I were looking out off the edge of the world. To the left were the calm, turquoise waters of the Indian Ocean and to the right were the rough, gray waters of the Atlantic. Directly in front of me these two great bodies collided, forming fascinating patterns of water movement. The shoreline was made of pure white sand crystals, against which the coarse, jagged cliffs formed almost a surrealistic contrast.

"With my first scan of the panorama, I was instantly overwhelmed with the realization that I was absorbing the most magnificent view I'd ever seen in my life. I wanted to shout but I couldn't because any additional noise would have defiled the solemn beauty. I wanted to fall on my knees under the weight of the awesomeness, but I didn't need to because I was already very much in touch with God. Instead, I did the only thing that seemed appropriate. It is something that I can't recall ever doing previously and yet at the time it seemed to be the only logical, rational, natural thing to do. Without forethought and without second thought, I reached into my pocket, took out a coin and scratched my wife's name on the rocks.

"How long it took—I have no idea. It didn't matter. I sculpted one letter at a time: M - A - R - L - E - N - E. Somehow when all the letters were completed I felt better. I looked at her name and then to the seascape, then back at her name again. Back and forth I gazed, almost hallucinating on the coalescence of these two awesome worlds—the view of the South African coastline and the thought of my wife back home. I knew that I would probably never return to that place, and most certainly not with my wife; but for a few seconds as I stood on the edge of the world, it was almost as if we enjoyed the moment together."

Dignity describes the marriage that takes our breath away. It's the thought of the most significant person in our life even when she is not physically present with us. It's the place in the center of our being that resonates with purpose and fulfillment, meaning, and significance. *Dignity* is what makes life worth living. It is the inner sanctum somewhere deep in a man's soul that indicates that we were created in the image of God. It's the essential element that separates us from the baboon. It is the desire we all have for people who know us best to be able to say at the end of our lives, "He was a good man." We may not accumulate a million dollars. We may not be seen on the front page of news magazine. But we had better be at the top of somebody's list of significant people, or we will feel a strange, hollow cavity inside our chest where our heart is supposed to be.

Dignity is what God destined for every married man—the man who puts his wife at the proper level of priority, and who plays by the rules. It is possible that your marriage may not be breathtaking. In fact, you may be working so hard to keep your marriage from falling apart that you are actually out of breath. That's okay. There is dignity for you, too. And some relief ahead.

Faithfulness Under Fire

This story from World War II is reportedly true. I have no way to verify it, but it's a good one.

The fighting was heavy. A platoon of U.S. troops was driven back and one of their infantrymen was wounded in gunfire. As he lay on the battlefield, a friend and fellow soldier asked his sergeant in the foxhole, "Can I go get 'im?"

"There's no use. He's probably dead," the sergeant answered. "And even if he isn't·dead, you'd never make it back alive. But if you want to . . ." Those last few words were all the friend needed to hear. Off he ran, dodging bullets. Crawling on elbows and knees, he reached the bleeding infantryman, hoisted him to his shoulders, and hobbled back. As he neared the foxhole, the heroic friend was hit in the chest with a bullet and the two friends collapsed in a heap. The sergeant tried to find the pulse of the infantryman and there was none. Dead. Then he told the soldier, "I told you it would be senseless. Your friend is dead, and now you've been shot." Fighting for air, the friend painfully explained, "No, I have no regrets. You see, when I first got to my friend he was alive. He recognized me and said, 'Thanks, Jack. I knew you'd come.'" With those words the soldier friend died.

That is friendship. Friendship says, "I knew you'd come"—*I knew if I needed you, you'd be there for me. I knew I could count on you.*

That is what makes a good marriage—not heroics but faithfulness under fire.

Faithfulness under fire is what every man longs for. It is love that keeps its word even when it hurts. It is the integrity that is just as loyal on a business trip halfway around the world as it is sitting at the breakfast table with our spouse. It is the inner sense of equilibrium that knows how to fight off the molesting demands of an overloaded schedule in order to maintain a man's commitments. When so many different fingers are scrambling to get into the control center of our lives and push our buttons, faithfulness is able to ward off the intruders bravely. This is the kind of love that has sticking power. It is the kind that will still be there twenty years later after the hairs turn gray and when the breasts sag, the belly is covered with stretch marks, and "cellulite" puts contours on the thighs. It will be there through the mood swings of menopause, the teenage children who forget the words "please" and "thank you," and the pains of the empty nest.

Faithfulness under fire is what separates a great marriage from a mediocre one. It is what every man and woman deep down longs for, but which very few seem to enjoy.

Friends

A husband and wife ought to be best friends. No one disagrees with the principle. But why is it that when a fat and sassy married couple sit on their love seat like overstuffed pillows and say, "We are best friends," it sounds like a hollow cliche? They look more like mannequins than real, live married people. While there is something inside every married person that wants to be best friends with their spouse, for many couples the words just don't ring true. They sound too syrupy, too storybook, too ethereal. How do we put real handles on this idea that we can all latch onto?

Kevin wanted to be friends with his wife, but it was not happening. They lived at the same address, ate at the same kitchen table. They even slept in the same bed. But friends they were not. His list of grievances sounded like this:

- "She is constantly late, and I hate to be late."

- "She is always out shopping, spending my hard-earned money."
- "She tells me she is always too tired to make love. I always feel like I'm begging for sex."
- "The other day she pulled her van out of the garage and scraped the whole side of my car—what an idiot!"
- "She gripes and complains constantly. She sounds like a leaky faucet."
- "She is always second-guessing my decisions. Indecision drives me loony-tunes."

Kevin growled about her—but underneath he freely admitted that he was very much in love with his wife. "I wouldn't still be married after twenty-seven years if I didn't love her," he told me.

As I listened carefully to Kevin, it was obvious that he was wrestling with his relationship, and I daresay he was losing. All the petty little grievances were like leeches sucking the lifeblood out of his marriage.

"Do these areas of irritation make you angry?" I asked rhetorically.

"They make me furious," he bellowed.

"They make you feel weak inside?" I asked.

I will never forget his next statement. "*Weak?* They make me feel castrated!"

The word *castrated* rattled around the room for a while. He felt frustrated, emasculated, impotent, dehumanized, dishonored, and he was hurting. Bleeding might be more like it.

That afternoon I shared with Kevin another of those principles that transformed my marriage: The principle of *yielding the right of way.*

Yield the Right of Way

Yielding the right of way not only works in traffic—it works wonders in marriage.

Yielding the right of way means voluntarily choosing to give up my personal desires in order to first meet the needs of my wife.

At first this principle sounds intimidating to the male psyche.

It's enough to turn our knuckles white with fear as we feel ourselves losing control. *If I do that,* you argue, *my wife will gain the upper hand. I thought I was supposed to be the leader in this relationship.* For any of us who have stock-piled heavy artillery over the years, the thought of turning lose territorial rights is similar to Israel giving up the Gaza Strip.

Relax. The key word is *voluntarily.* We want to be heroes, not robots. No one holds a gun to the head of a hero. Heroes respond out of *want to.* When they see a friend lying in his own blood out on the battlefield of life, they instantly scan the possibilities, compute the risks, and voluntarily make a choice to become involved.

Every day, every husband faces real life battlefields where he has the opportunity to lay down his life for his wife. It usually does not involve anything sensational or physically life-threatening. Usually, the day-to-day situations we face are far less spectacular.

- Not every man will run out into heavy traffic to snatch his wife a split second before she's hit by an oncoming bus . . .
  —but every husband has the opportunity to adjust his schedule and make time to help his wife with some of the overwhelming domestic duties of life before she is crushed by an oncoming deadline.
- Not every man will lunge himself into the line of fire to protect his wife from the bullets of an assault rifle . . .
  —but every husband will have opportunity to help his wife deal with hurtful criticism and reckless words.
- Not every husband will be able to rescue his wife from drowning at sea after falling overboard . . .
  but every husband will be able to encourage his wife when she feels overwhelmed by the domestic needs and about to suffocate from her own low self-esteem.
- Not every husband will run through flames and pull his wife from a smoke-filled room . . .
  —but when wives are unable to see clearly in the face of critical decisions, every husband is able to lay aside his personal rights and attempt to put her needs first.

Each of these corresponding options involves sacrifice. They each, in some way, call for the husband to lay down his life. The situations are not as dramatic as the physically life-threatening ones. They will not become material for the latest TV mini-series. But they are what give men dignity in the everyday of marriage.

Every man has a deep desire to be a hero. It is not that we necessarily have a flair for the dramatic, but when called upon in the line of duty, we want to be found faithful—even if that means laying down our lives. Our problem is that heroes never choose the arena for their own heroics. A hero doesn't wake up in the morning and say over his oatmeal, "I'm going to risk my life today in the line of duty."

Life-threatening situations do not come knocking with a neon sign flashing that says, "Choose me. I'll make you a hero." Instead, while minding our own business, there comes an opportunity to lay aside personal preference, and it's then we can voluntarily rise to the occasion. Husbands become heroes by responding with bravery to the day-to-day normal load of husbanding.

Out of a sense of desperation, Kevin was motivated to relieve the stress in his marriage. He was weary from years of locking horns over petty issues, and he knew something had to change. But Kevin was defeated and tired. "I'm sick of the whole thing. I feel like I've been giving in to her my whole life."

"There's a significant difference," I told Kevin, "between *yielding the right of way* and *giving in*." It's like this:

- *Giving in* is an expression of defeat.
  —*Yielding the right of way* is an expression of love.
- *Giving in* is hopeless—it expects no response at all.
  —*Yielding the right of way* hopes that the love demonstrated will eventually change the heart of the one receiving the favor.
- *Giving in* is the result of seeing no other options.
  —*Yielding the right of way* is a choice of our own free will.
- *Giving in* places the person in further bondage.
  —*Yielding the right of way* sets free the person who does the yielding.
- *Giving in* removes respect from everyone.

—*Yielding the right of way* extends dignity to everyone involved.
- *Giving in* is what makes prisoners of war.
  —*Yielding the right of way* is what makes heroes.
- *Giving in* focuses on the irritating surface situation.
  —*Yielding the right of way* focuses on the underlying personal right we are voluntarily laying aside.

Kevin was in bondage. He was defeated. He had not been showing respect to his wife and he had not been receiving much back. It was time for a change.

A Huge 3×5 Card

Kevin wanted to see past his surface problems. His relationship needed to move beyond *she-did-this-to-me* knee-jerk reactions, and he was asking for help.

I handed him a 3×5 card and asked him to draw a line down the middle forming two columns. The left-hand column represented the surface situations that irritated him in his marriage. That column was easy for him to complete. Then I asked him to list in the right-hand column the corresponding personal rights that had been violated and that caused him to become irritated. This was a bit more difficult for him to understand. Eventually he caught on.

His list looked like this:

My Angry Situation	*My Personal Right*
My wife is always late.	To be on time.
She buys a new dress.	To spend my own money.
She refuses to make love.	To have sex when I want it.
She scrapes the side of my new car.	To drive a car that looks new.
She gripes and complains, chronically—like a leaky faucet.	For her to honor me.
She always second-guesses my decisions.	To have her support.

I then asked Kevin a question that seemed to rattle his fillings. "Do you love your wife enough to give up your personal desires in order to meet her needs first?" He sat there stunned, so I rephrased the question. "Do you love your wife enough to voluntarily lay aside your personal rights? To never demand or fight for those territorial rights again?" As Kevin sat across the room with those questions echoing in his masculine soul, I knew he was wrestling with years of contrary behavior that would not easily turn loose. He was weighing the possibility of tearing down walls that he spent years building. He sat at the crossroads where every husband sits. The place where paths diverge in the middle of life, where the ultimate issues are settled—issues like, *What would I do if it came right down to who gets the parachute?* Only for Kevin it was not a parachute. Neither was it money nor sex nor being on time. For Kevin and for every man the real issue is love. *Whom do I really love? My wife or myself?*

The Love Factor

The love factor is well captured in the words of Jesus: "Greater love has no one than this, that one lay down his life for his friends" (John 15:13). We quote Jesus not to sound pious but to give credit where credit is due. He stands head and shoulders above anyone else in history when it comes to putting others first. Even though He was never married, we as husbands have no better role model. In fact, according to the Bible, Jesus was intended to be a husband's role model. As we read earlier, Paul reminds us: "Husbands, love your wives, just as Christ loved the church and gave himself up for her" (Ephesians 5:25). Notice the specific love factor highlighted is that element of giving of himself sacrificially. Elsewhere, in one of the most profound pieces of poetry found anywhere in literature, we read about the direct connection between the love factor and yielding the right of way. Feast your eyes:

> Your attitude should be the kind that was shown us by Jesus Christ who, though he was God, did not demand or cling to his rights as God, but laid aside his mighty power and glory,

taking the disguise of a slave and becoming like men. And he humbled himself even further, going so far as actually to die a criminal's death on a cross.

Philippians 2:5–8, TLB

There is one overriding characteristic of *the love factor*. It does not cling to its own personal rights. This is seen nowhere as clearly as it is in Jesus.

"Kevin," I asked a second time, "are you willing to demonstrate your love for your wife by voluntarily giving up that list of personal rights and desires in order to meet her needs first?"

I can still remember his response that evening. We were at his home in front of a roaring fire. He looked across the room and said, "I'll do it." He stood up, walked straight across the floor, grabbed a handful of tinder and, as he named every single personal right, he threw a piece of wood on the fire. "I die to my right to be on time," he said as he tossed a stick into the fire. "I give up my right to have sex when I want it," and he tossed another. When his list was relinquished, he took the 3×5 card and threw that on the flames as well. After looking into the flames for several moments, he looked over at me with a spirit of adventure in his countenance I had not seen before. "I already feel lighter—like a free man."

Friends

Learning to yield the right of way is not a singular decision, made in front of a fire once in a lifetime. It is a daily decision to be made every time we hit turbulence and voluntarily choose to put our wives first. It is a means of saying *I love you* in a language wives understand. The purpose is not simply to avoid conflict, but rather to communicate kindness. Every time a husband feels his temper rising because of an oncoming potential marital conflict, no flags wave. No siren goes off. No bells ring. No whistles blow. But smart men train themselves to look beyond the surface irritation and ask, *Which of my personal rights has been violated? How can I give up my preference in order to meet her needs first?*

A husband who chooses to yield the right of way will never accumulate a trophy case full of marital merit badges, purple hearts, or wall plaques. Chances are he won't even get honorable mention at the county fair. There is, however, a department store full of intangibles that this man will tap into which a lesser man will only dream about.

- *Friendship* grows out of sacrifice. A husband who gives up his own personal preferences in order to put his wife first will win her friendship, loyalty, trust, and devotion. Any woman would have to be deranged who would walk away from a husband like that.
- *A clear conscience* is perhaps even a greater benefit. When a husband voluntarily chooses to please his wife, he will not always get his way but he will always be able to sleep well at night.
- *Freedom from anger* is a pleasant by-product of giving up our personal rights. As we give over the control of our lives to God, we are free from the crushing weight of anxiety and a wicked temper. We can say, *God, I have given up those rights to you. I will let you settle the score.*
- *Peaceful communication* flows from yielded personal rights. We no longer engage in head-butting, manipulating, or intimidating. We are now free to talk about issues instead of forcing them.

It has been twelve years since Kevin and I sat in front of his fireplace. We are still "Christmas card" friends. When he learned I was writing a book on marriage he phoned me. "Tell them about the love factor—encourage them to yield the right of way. They will never be sorry. It completely changed the atmosphere of our home. At first I felt like I was committing political suicide. It felt like everything was spinning out of control. Little did I know that for the first time in our marriage, we would genuinely learn how to love each other. I can honestly say my wife would now do anything for me. Our arguments have virtually ended. Hey, once in a while I still have to die to my own rights the way Jesus did for me, but I don't mind. It's the least I can do for my wife, compared to all she does for me."

As I listened to my friend, I knew I was listening to a voice of experience—a man who learned to give up his personal rights in order to demonstrate love to his wife; and he was not only savoring the benefits, he was walking in the light of dignity.

Duty without dignity is deadly. But as you can see, duty *with* dignity is delightful. Now let's zoom in on this virtue called dignity and take a closer look.

The Winner's Circle

As I watched the final moments of a PGA Tournament, I learned more about life than I did about golf. The winner was in the tent signing his score card and, to everyone's amazement, he added one stroke to his score, moving him out of a tie for first place and reducing his prize money by $30,000. Everyone was shocked.

"Why did you add a stroke to your score?" a sportscaster inquired. "You would have been tied for first."

"Yes," the golfer explained, "but my putter hit the ball, causing it to roll a fraction of an inch. That should rightfully be counted as a stroke."

"But no one saw it happen. No one would ever have known," an official commented.

"No, that is not true," the professional golfer qualified. "Someone saw it. I saw it—and so did my son."

No one asked any more questions. They didn't need to. They walked away in silent admiration for a man who chose to stand in the real winner's circle as a man of virtue.

Every man longs to spend a few moments in such a winner's circle. He doesn't need a Pulitzer Prize, induction into the Hall of Fame, or first place in a PGA Tournament. But he does need to know that he's honored by those who are closest to him. He needs to feel the inner fulfillment of knowing he rings true to those who know him best. And if a man fails to spend time there, he might as well have never lived.

This morning's paper reminded me of a statistic I have read before. Some 27,000 Americans commit suicide every year, and 75% of them are men. Why? Could it be that they are the ones who are not finding dignity? Could it be that in the face of feminism, men are not quite sure where they fit in? Surely a man does not make a deliberate choice to live without dignity. More likely some of us are just looking for it in the wrong places.

The Right Places

A man is destined for dignity. Dignity is the baton of value we pass on to our children and grandchildren that enables us to outlive ourselves. It's something none of us was born with—instead, it's an invaluable gift we acquire as we live with consistency. It comes to the man who is characterized by the virtues of integrity, sensitivity, humility, responsibility, fidelity, and charity. In our day these virtues are a highly classified group, a select breed. We have already looked at them in isolation, but now without any marching band or 21-gun salute, let's line them up in single file and do roll call. As we do so, we will be redefining manhood and pointing the way to the real winner's circle.

Integrity

Integrity is who we are when no one else is watching. It is who we are when the TV cameras are not running, when the doors are closed and the lights are out. Integrity knows respect that no amount of money can buy. It does not compromise convictions to fit the circumstances, it owes no apologies, it is not auctioned off to the highest bidder. A man of integrity is a man of honor.

The definition of *integrity* in Webster's New World Dictionary sounds bland, but it is helpful. "The quality of being complete; unbroken; entirety; being of sound moral principle." The root word comes from their Latin word *integritas,* which means "wholeness." The mathematical term *integer* means "intact, entire, complete in itself," as opposed to a fraction. All of this indicates that a person of integrity is a person who is unified, whole, complete—one who *has it all together.*

The opposite of integrity is *duplicity,* which means to be double-minded, to have split motivation, or to be deceptive or hypocritical. This represents a man with a fragmented inner life, who has no unifying principles to rally around, no central value system by which to determine right from wrong, and who is therefore pulled in a multitude of different directions. Such a man offers poor leadership to his wife and children. This does not mean that he is necessarily hypocritical and phoney. It means that because of his split motivation, he will appear inconsistent. It is no wonder the Bible observes that "a double-minded man will be unstable in all his ways" (see James 1:5–6).

Whether we play on the PGA tour, or settle for croquet in the backyard, integrity is vital to every game in life. Integrity gives a man's life a rudder by which he can maintain direction as he navigates the storms of life. By integrity, he can provide consistency, stability, and discernment for those under his leadership. It will not necessarily improve our score, but it will certainly improve our marriage and our other significant relationships.

- By integrity a man with many interests and responsibilities will be able to maintain focus and direction without being pulled off course.
- A man of integrity is a good decision maker, able to discern the needs of a situation according to a consistent value system.
- A man of integrity is able to build lasting friendships. He himself has a clear conscience and is more trusting of others, and those around him find him trustworthy.

Sensitivity

For more than a generation, Hollywood has elevated men who never display a tender cell in their bodies. Our fathers watched rough, tough John Wayne who rode into town on horseback having been away for weeks, looked his woman straight in the eye and said in his deep, expressionless voice, "Hey, Tootsie, what's for dinner?" Not very sensitive. Many of us have more recently been raised with a similar, aloof male role model—James Bond. For him, a woman was a plaything, an opponent to beat at mind games, a sex object to conquer. Again, sensitivity was not his style. Put these two movie stars together, and we realize that we've been looking up to masculine prototypes who have not been setting a good example for the rest of us.

If integrity represents the straight side of manly virtue, sensitivity represents the soft side. But don't misunderstand. Soft does not mean mushy, mild, or milquetoast. There is great strength in the virtue of sensitivity. There is almost a strange dichotomy in the qualities of a mature man. On the one hand he is bold, focused, decisive. On the other hand he is broken, tenderhearted and vulnerable. Our society has done everything conceivable to compartmentalize these two character traits into irreconcilable categories. *If a man is tender, he cannot be firm,* or so we think.

A man who is hardened, calloused, or impenetrable is often desperately trying to protect the little man inside. Insecurity and inferiority often mask themselves behind a macho-man facade. Hard outer shells are fine for turtles, but they don't fit men. A real man is not afraid to show his own feelings or to identify with the feelings of others. This is a big pill for some men to swallow.

Jesus was a mature man, and the record shows us that He experienced the full range of emotion. He was referred to as a man of sorrows and acquainted with grief, and yet He could party with the best of them, known as a friend of sinners, gluttons, and winos. We're told that because of all Jesus has been through, He is able to sympathize with us in all our weaknesses and with all our emotions. He is able to vibrate with our highest exhilaration and our deepest grief. He feels with us at every level. As men, when we mature we develop a similar ability to not only experience the full range of emotional response, but to be touched by the emotions of others who are close to us.

Sensitivity is something we don't need to be afraid of. It wins us far more points than we will ever realize to feel with our wife, to emotionally lock on to the same wavelength. Too many women would rather have twelve minutes of genuine compassion from their husbands than a dozen roses.

When a man is sensitive to his wife, she feels loved and cherished. It says to her,

- "I care."
- "I understand you."
- "The way you feel about things is important to me."
- "You are not alone."
- "I am standing with you."

A man who chooses sensitivity will feel the risks. We might as well admit it. They are, however, a risk worth taking. No matter how alien this character trait may seem, sensitivity is part of mature manhood and is part of a healthy marriage.

Humility

No one was born humble. We might have been born white or black, American, French, or Lithuanian. We might have been born into humble circumstances with limited financial resources, but we do not inherit true humility of spirit from anyone. It is not that easy. True humility is a choice we make—a choice to be made every day.

This is the most elusive character trait. Like a bar of soap, just the moment we think, *I have a good grip on humility,* it squirts out of our hands. Or as the cartoon states, "I used to be proud. But now that I have that under control, I'm perfect." Not so fast.

We have already illustrated the offensive nature of pride and have presented a tangible method of choosing humility—by yielding the right of way. There's just one problem. It ain't easy. John Bunyan said in his classic *Pilgrim's Progress,* "It is a very hard matter for a man to go down into the valley of humiliation." We fight it tooth and nail. We may read words about choosing the low road and sit there and smile. We may relax in our easy chair and hear about washing our wife's feet and think, *Piece of cake.* But when it comes time to bend in front of our wife, inside we spit and sputter.

Even though it cuts across the grain of every cell in our body, we need to understand that humility does more than simply re-move the great threat of pride from our marriage. It opens up to us the greatest honor imaginable. Even if you share no religious convictions, just suppose the Bible contains some wisdom. Listen to what it says about the enormous virtues of humility:

- God opposes the proud, but gives grace to the humble (James 4:6).
- Humble yourselves, therefore, under the mighty hand of God, that he may lift you up in due time (1 Peter 5:6).
- Humility comes before honor (Proverbs 15:33).
- With humility comes wisdom (Proverbs 11:2).
- For whoever exalts himself will be humbled, and whoever humbles himself will be exalted (Matthew 23:12).

Unlike other virtues, humility never gets any easier. It never comes naturally. It will always involve a voluntary choice which at the moment will seem senseless. Idiotic. It will feel frustrating. Contradictory. But the low road is always the way that leads to dignity.

Humility scores points. A wife loves to hear humility speak. She loves to hear words like:

- "I am willing to wait until tomorrow night."
- "I forgive you."
- "I will adjust my schedule."
- "Here, let me help you."
- "It's okay. I'm willing to do it your way."
- "No. I refuse to blast you with my explosive temper. Let me walk away, cool down, and communicate my feelings in a few minutes."

There is no man alive who will ever nibble on a single pinch of dignity without learning to walk through the valley of humil-iation. On the other side of the bleachers, we need to admit humility will not usually win a standing ovation either. We will not drive home and spot a billboard on the thruway that reads: "Honey, I appreciate your humility!" It is a virtue without fan-fare. And because we as men rarely pay tribute to quiet heroes, we fail to give this super hero—humility—a fair shake. Too bad.

Chances are, there is one special lady who is waiting for us to wake up and realize just what we have been missing.

Humility is the quality in a man that makes it possible for his wife to pay tribute. Without it she feels he is too busy praising himself.

Boasting is always a bad idea. No sooner do the self-inflating words get out of our mouth than they fall flat to the ground. They may have been the precise words our wife was about to say, but now that we have said them, they will not mean quite as much coming from our spouse's mouth like an echo. Sincere compliments that are the most encouraging are always spontaneous. No matter how much we want our wife to notice a kind deed or brag about our superior achievements, priming the pump is self-defeating. In fact, when we are silently craving a compliment, rather than drawing attention to what we have done, it is always a preferred gesture to give a sincere compliment. Any honor we give to our wives will in one way or another come back to benefit us anyway.

Humility enables a man to be a better husband. It is not in your husbandly job description to be perfect, but you do need to communicate to your wife that you are attempting to become a better husband.

A spirit of humility gives hope to any marriage. Humility puts a husband's heart next to his wife's heart, no matter where she is. It is the doorway that takes us into the chambers of sensitivity and on into all the other winsome virtues—pride is the wall that keeps us out.

Responsibility

Maturity says, *I'm responsible—you can hold me accountable.* No matter how effective or ineffective we may be at a task, if we are willing to stand up and assume proper responsibility for our actions, it will win more respect than if we pass the buck or try to hide.

A professional athlete looks a teammate in the eye after a failed play, pats his own chest, and mouths the words, "My bad!" Enough said. It doesn't matter if he dropped a pass in the end zone, or missed a lay-up in the NBA, when a player admits his own mistake, he regains acceptance. Dead issue. If, however, he tries to make excuses, watch out! Tempers flare. Attitudes sharpen. Tension builds. For both athletes and husbands, it is a good idea to learn to say at the appropriate moments, "My bad!"

"My bad" is not the only way to assume responsibility. When we are willing to stoop to assume responsibility for failure, this also opens up the door to be able to assume partial responsibility for success. There is an inner fulfillment that we can enjoy when we assume responsibility.

The desire to hold responsibility is as built into a man as the desire to fly is built into a bird. The movement from infancy to manhood can be charted on the continuum of assuming responsibility. In our first moment of life, we breathe for ourselves. Then we eat for ourselves. Then walk for ourselves. We tie our own shoes. Before long we find ourselves in the middle of our teenage years, fighting for independence and responsibility. We want to decide how loud we play our music, how long we wear our hair, and how late we stay out on weekends. Sooner than we anticipate, we pick a college, career, life partner, and everything begins to snowball. With children, house payments, taxes, utility bills, we feel as if we are wearing more hats than Bo Jackson or Deion Sanders. We feel like crawling into the foxhole and hoisting up the sign, "Off duty."

Inside, we feel like running away from the weariness of duty without dignity. And yet something else reminds us that there is no dignity without responsibility.

From the moment that God gave man the initial nod to be fruitful and multiply, the twin towers of dignity and responsibility were cemented together. This is precisely why there is a built-in desire in man to assume responsibility.

When a man stands up and says, *I'm responsible for my wife and children. Yes, you can hold me accountable,* he becomes eligible for a level of dignity he will find nowhere else. The man who dares to pat his chest and at times say "My bad" is the one who will also receive countless pats on the back from his wife and children. And, far more significantly, he is the man who will one day stand before his Maker and hear Him say, "Well done, good and faithful servant. You've done well with your responsibilities" (Matthew 25:21).

There will always be times when a man feels like running out from under the weight of all his responsibilities. We might as well admit it, though—for a man to run from responsibility is to run from reality. Sooner or later it will catch up to him and leave him feeling hollow inside. But on the other hand, the place of inner fulfillment and true dignity—where a man longs to stand in honor—is found in the everyday of life. It is the man who sticks with the stuff and who takes his turn with diapers and child discipline who will savor the richness of his own manhood.

Fidelity

The longest month of my life was the month before I was married. I was in New Jersey and my bride-to-be was in Grand Rapids, Michigan. Bummer! The long-distance company may advertise "Reach out and touch someone," but that was not exactly my experience. I found talking to be an inadequate substitute for touching. I was a virgin, by the grace of God, and Sherry was a virgin, but we were both physically healthy young adults with hormones that at times felt hyperactive. Nonetheless, we had sexually saved ourselves for each other, and we were committed to maintain that trust into our marriage. Therefore, I decided to creatively use this opportunity to memorize and meditate on a chapter from the Bible. This gets comical.

The words I learned included these:

> Drink water from your own cistern,
> running water from your own well.
> Should your springs overflow in the streets,
> your streams of water in public squares?
> Let them be yours alone,
> never to be shared with strangers.
> May your fountain be blessed,
> and may you rejoice in the wife of your youth.
> A loving doe, a graceful deer—

may her breasts satisfy you always,
may you ever be captivated by her love.
—Proverbs 5:15–20

At the time, I assure you I was relishing the thought of being satisfied always by *her breasts,* being captivated, enthralled, mesmerized, self-engrandized *by her love.* Frankly, I found all such anticipation quite fulfilling and perfectly righteous. I knew that even though we were not yet married, I was in no danger since she was a thousand miles away. And the next time we'd see each other we would walk the aisle together. I reasoned: *The verse says, "The wife of your youth." So I'd better enjoy these verses while I'm young, because she won't be young for much longer.*

Twenty years later I'm still satisfied with her breasts—quite sincerely, more satisfied than ever. And I'm even more captivated by her love. In addition I have become a better Bible student. The verse says, "The wife of your youth." It does not say, *Your young wife.* What this means is, no matter how many years we've been married, she is still "the wife of my youth." Even when we have been married forty, fifty, sixty years or more, she will still be the wife of my youth.

After my wife has suffered the wear and tear of having babies, midnight feedings, grocery shopping, fixing meals, waxing floors, chauffeuring children, vacuuming, facilitating the family budget, and the cumulative effect of living with a guy like me for all these years, I do not run off with a younger model. I don't trade in my fifties' wife with stretch marks and loss of muscle tone to get some nineties' model. No way. As long as I am married to the bride I married, I will always be able to roll over in the morning, look into her face and say, "How is the wife of my youth?"

I still ask my bride that question. She enjoys it. For her it's an opportunity to hear her husband tell her that she is still the twinkle in his eye. For me it's my way to reaffirm my commitment to monogamy and to say, *I'm married, and I'm not looking.*

My neighbor drives to work every day in a car with a bumper sticker I admire: "I love my wife." The other day I asked him, "Where did you get it?" He just smiled, and then added the obvious, "My wife gave it to me." She gave it to him, but he decided to put it on his bumper. Smart choice.

We do not all need to wear it on our bumper, but we need to put it somewhere for all to see: "I love my wife."

At our wedding Sherry gave me a ring I loved but soon outgrew. For years I did not wear a wedding ring and thought little of it. I was married, I was very much in love, and I felt no motivation to wear a wedding band. At least, not until I began traveling more frequently and I was propositioned several times on airplanes, in restaurants, and in motel lobbies. When I noticed this potentially dangerous pattern, I took Sherry to a local jeweler and together we selected an appropriate wedding band. Now I not only wear the wedding band, but at every opportunity, I say something nice about my wife in public. I don't have a bumper sticker, but I still use every opportunity to say, "I love my wife."

Let's be candid: Wearing a wedding ring has little to do with fidelity. Fidelity goes deeper than even being sexually faithful to our wives. Some men have never physically violated that commitment, but they are pornography addicts, committing mental adultery every chance they have. That is being a phony. A fantasy life that is unfaithful snatches more dignity from men than all the one-night stands put together. True fidelity saves its thoughts as well as its love exclusively for the wife of your youth.

Charity

Charity is love with legs—love in action; love that gives itself away. In a sense, it is the sum total of all these virtues braided together into a single strand. It is the *summum bonum* of life—the highest good. When it is all said and done, love is the only facet of life that will stand the test of time. When the Bible says, "The greatest gift is love," it is not overstating the case (1 Corinthians 13:13). When Jesus said, "The whole law is fulfilled in love," He was not oversimplifying things. When the apostle Paul said, "The goal of this command is love," he was not exaggerating. Love is the essence of life. It is the wood in the fireplace, the food on the table, the roof over our heads, the wind in our sails, the money in the bank of every marriage.

In high school, I was a card-carrying bachelor. *I will never settle down with one woman,* I was convinced. Several years later, after only two months of dating Sherry, I was scared spitless over the four-word question that wouldn't leave my mind: *Will you marry me?* Don't misunderstand. I wouldn't dare say the words, but even thinking them was causing my hair to fall out. I went to the nearest pay phone and called my dad. I rambled. I quoted all the late-night, threadbare logic my roommates and I discussed, laying out the pluses and minuses of our relationship. I spoke of backgrounds, personality, economics, temperaments, schooling, career, timing. When I eventually ran out of words, I asked my dad, "So what do you think?" I was expecting some profound, elaborate philosophical marital insight. He fooled me. He asked me one simple question: "Do you love her?"

Do I love her, I thought. *What a childish question! Don't you have anything profound to say?* I was expecting something deep and elaborate from my dad. After several moments of silence, he asked again, "Do you love her?"

Didn't he know I was facing a life or death issue? I nervously chuckled. Then I repeated, " 'Do I love her?'—Dad, are you suggesting that that's the big question I need to ask at a moment like this?"

Then he chuckled, and he handed me one of those pearls of wisdom over the telephone that dads are famous for. "Fred, if you love her, everything else will take care of itself."

Standing in that phone booth, those words echoed in my mind as if a bomb exploded. I realized I was taken to the bottom line faster than I wanted. I would have preferred some sophisticated answer that I could grapple with mentally. But this love stuff went far deeper. Somehow I knew it would cost me everything.

It was another eight months before I asked Sherry to marry me, but that afternoon I realized I was free to continue to pursue the relationship as long as it was being motivated by genuine love—*charity.*

———

Since genuine love is so explosive, so costly, so dangerous, we will spread it out carefully in the next chapter. It's the one element that every marriage requires and yet so few enjoy. Proceed at your own risk.

Fresh Air

Every home needs fresh air. At times we suffocate for lack of it—physically and emotionally. Yet it's surprising how many husbands live with the emotional windows closed.

Early in our marriage, I was in my office trying to complete a project within deadline. My creative juices were frozen. I think I read the same sentence nine times. *What is the problem?* I thought. *Why am I stuck in the mud when it's only the middle of the morning?* I got up from my chair, walked over, opened the window, and then attempted to resume studying, hoping that an increase in the oxygen to my brain would help stimulate my thinking.

It did not help. I got desperate. *Lord, please! I have a deadline and I need some help,* I prayed. *I'll do anything.*

A new idea popped into my mind. *You were at odds with Sherry when you left the house. You spoke with her harshly. You were insensitive. If you expect to get any creative work done, you need to first set things straight at home.* (It's amazing the brilliant insights we can have after we pray.)

I followed the impulse, took an early lunch break, and went home to ask for forgiveness. It was a good thing I did. Sherry had been crying. We hugged. We touched hearts. "Yes, I forgive you," she assured me. We made spirit-to-spirit contact. And we were reconciled.

That afternoon when I returned to my office, the air was still unusually stuffy despite the fact that the window had been wide open for over an hour. It was then I noticed that the outer storm window was shut. I shook my head. *You idiot!* As soon as it slid open, the crisp Massachusetts air invigorated my work area. I was able to resume progress and, as you might suspect, that afternoon I was able to complete my project. But more importantly, I found myself on center stage in a living allegory. Follow this with me.

That storm window represented something far more to me than simply a winter protective shield. It represented my wife's spirit. When I arrived at my office that morning, not only was the air in the room stuffy, but so was the atmosphere in my marriage. My wife's spirit was shut up as tight as the storm window. Even when I attempted to improve the environment by throwing open the window, I was stymied. My life's work was on hold until I resolved my marital conflict. But once Sherry and I were reconciled in our spirits, and our internal windows were both thrown open wide, I was then able to facilitate my project.

Before I left my office that evening, I reached for a Bible on the shelf. Words I had read before were now filled with a reservoir of new meaning. "Husbands, in the same way be considerate as you live with your wives, and treat them with respect as the weaker partner and as heirs with you of the gracious gift of life, so that nothing will hinder your prayers" (1 Peter 3:7). Gushing with new significance in light of my fresh experience, I reread the words: *partner . . . as heirs with you of the gracious gift of life.*

The gracious gift of life represented fresh air. And the *partner . . . heirs with you* represented the pair of windows that must cooperate together. No longer am I simply a single person who can throw open his own window at will and expect results regardless of what I've done to my wife's spiritual and emotional condition. Now that we are married and have been mysteriously fused together, I must operate in tandem with her. Preserving this unity of spirit is vital to the health of every loving marriage. Fresh air is at stake and we won't survive long without it.

It is a man's responsibility to make sure his home has plenty of spiritual fresh air. This is one of the most challenging responsibilities that a man has—to make sure that his spirit is clean and unhindered toward his wife, and to make sure she is open and pure-hearted toward him. It is fresh air that allows the home to be a creative environment of love, joy, peace, and fulfillment. It is fresh air that wards off diseases like bitterness, jealousy, pride, immorality, greed, selfishness, and other malignancies that potentially molest our marriage. It is fresh air that captures the imagination of our children and makes them prefer returning home rather than wandering off somewhere else. It is fresh air that fills our lungs with laughter and enables our eyes to see the issues of life more clearly.

Maintaining a clean atmosphere is no little task.

Domestic Duties

Halitosis is the medical term for bad breath. *Housatosis* is the marital term for bad attitude. It is the foul odor that permeates everything when a husband and wife get sour toward each other. Uncovering the source of the smell is often tricky business. Neglected domestic duties cause a stench that is nauseating to wives and at times not even noticeable to men. A woman whose role is primarily homemaker is constantly provoked by the chipped paint and dripping faucet, while the husband who spends nine hours every workday outside the home sometimes couldn't care less. This makes for a nasty dose of *housatosis*.

What makes things even worse is that wives thrive on a little thing called order. It is one of those little invisible areas of a home that can easily be overlooked. On a scale of one to ten, wives usually rank the irritation of disorder in the home toward the top of the list. A man can walk into his home, sidestep the squabbles, maneuver the mayhem, overlook chaos, sit down and eat his dinner without indigestion. Not his wife. She feels ruptures in relationships more readily. She is upset by any turbulence. A wife likes an orderly filing system, orderly correspondence, orderly and reconciled bank statements, orderly budgeting, an orderly weekly schedule, and a well-ordered living environment.

"You never do anything around the house," Sherry complained to me a few years ago when I was charging into the office every spare moment to finish a project. Her words rang with a startling tinge of exasperation.

"Like what?" I innocently asked.

She rattled off a dozen domestic duties that hammered me like an Uzi submachine gun: "Screen door. Driveway. Leaky faucet. Gutters. Weedeating. Garage. Dog flops. Bushes." She probably could have kept going, but I interrupted.

"All right. Enough." I must admit, I *had* heard her mention these before but had not given it a second thought. Now the squeaky wheel had my full attention. The problem was I had dug myself into such a hole, I had no idea how to climb out of it. So, I did the only proper husbandly thing to do. I walked away!

Twenty minutes later I came back, climbed way out on a limb, handed her a legal pad and freely solicited all the domestic duties she could think of. "Please. I want you to write down every job you see that needs to be done around the house, and I promise to do them all—just give me two months."

Boy—talk is cheap! When I said those words, I had no idea what I had gotten myself into. I completely put myself at her mercy.

She smiled with the grin of a Cheshire cat and took me up on my proposal. She wrote down twenty-eight chores. I read the list and felt as if I had been sentenced to life imprisonment. *I'll never get done,* I thought.

That first week I did two jobs and I felt as if I'd swum the English Channel. The second week I did five and it wasn't too bad. The third week I went nuts. Something got into me and I completed fifteen jobs in one day. I was so proud of myself when it was all done, I took my camcorder and videotaped the entire sequence of events. I filmed the front lawn, back lawn, grass clippings bagged and at the curb, edging, fertilizing, overseeding, weather stripping, repaired wall socket, weedeating, shrub trimming, cultivating and sweeping. I even resurfaced the driveway with asphalt sealant. It has gone down in the Hartley family history as one of our funniest home videos. But when we watch it, I must admit no one else seems to enjoy it quite as much as I do.

At the end of eight weeks, every chore was done. I not only checked off my complete *honey-do list,* but I received the greater sense of satisfaction watching my wife's expressions change. She loved watching my zealous performance, but even more she enjoyed all the TLC she received. Order to our home brought order to her heart. Only then, after all the chores were complete, I discovered the intimate connection between caring for my home and caring for my wife. Not all of us are destined to be the Ace-hardware man, but we all can change light bulbs. Most importantly, we can change our attitude.

It made me feel good to do something so simple that brought such joy. It was exciting to gain such influx of emotional and spiritual fresh air in our home as a result of such a slight shift in my own priorities. The bottom-line factor that motivates me to do the domestic duties is not simply the fact that every duty is saying, "Honey, I love you." Quite honestly, there are times when I pick rotten leaves out of the gutter when I feel no love whatsoever for my wife. But the factor that motivates me to complete domestic duties is the fact that every duty is saying, *"Jesus, I love you."* Ultimately, I know that loving my wife is pleasing to my Maker. Whether my love is being expressed by picking up dog flops in the backyard or fixing the caulking around the bathtub, it is all worship to my God because it translates love into tangibles my wife can understand.

What I'm saying is this: Too often we segregate our lives into the *sacred* and the *secular.* We erect a Berlin Wall between the areas God might be involved in and all the rest of life that is considered my responsibility. That shallow view of life has destroyed more men than the Vietnam war. It is time to tear down the wall and declare to the world that all of life is sacred. God is active in every area, and we are able to enjoy His involvement in the yard on Saturday afternoon as well as in the bedroom after hours.

There is no fresher, cleaner air than the fresh breath of God in a home. When a man learns to be tender and considerate of his wife, it pleases God. When a man begins to treat his wife as an equal and not as an inferior being, when he opens himself to share his true feelings with her and when he pours himself out to serve her, he can even sense God's pleasure. And the sense of His pleasure is the sweetest fragrance a man will ever inhale. That is rare air.

A couple of Bible verses have permanently stapled this thought to my mind and heart:

- "Therefore, I urge you, in view of God's mercy, to offer your bodies as living sacrifices, holy and pleasing to God—which is your spiritual [act of] worship" (Romans 12:1). I now realize that whenever I fulfill a domestic duty for Sherry, I am engaging in a spiritual act of worship. Beyond simply saying, *Sherry, I love you,* I am in fact saying, *Jesus, I love you.* This is where marriage takes on its fuller dimension. This is where I can get air beyond the flight of even Michael Jordan.

- "And whatever you do, whether in word or in deed, do it all in the name of the Lord Jesus, giving thanks to God the Father through him" (Colossians 3:17). When I am expected to do a household chore that I do not particularly relish, these words come to mind. The exhortation to do it all in the name of Jesus—for His pleasure and for His credit—and to do it with a cheerful heart have kept me from a bad attitude hundreds of times.

Everything Stinks

It's one thing to have a bad day. But when a sequence of bad days gets strung together, it seems as though everything in life is going wrong. The car breaks down, our teenager brings home a lousy report card, there is talk of a layoff at work, the hot-water heater leaks, the wife is cranky—and then we discover that even our chest hairs are turning gray.

When everything in life smells bad to me, I remember the little story about limburger cheese. The old man slept in the den, and his children played a trick on him. They rubbed limburger cheese in his mustache. Some time later he awoke complaining the couch smelled bad. He stood up, walked across the room, sat down in his lounge chair, and soon determined that the room stunk. He walked into the living room and announced that the whole house stank. Seeing no other options, he walked outside, took a deep breath—and could hardly believe his nostrils! Frustrated, he declared, "The whole world stinks!"

The moral to the story is simple: When it seems as though the whole world stinks, the problem is most likely right under our own nose. And when it seems that the whole world stinks, it usually is not limburger cheese in our mustache. More likely, what causes the air of our lives to smell is usually our own attitude toward life and how we feel toward ourselves.

Fact: A man treats his wife the way he feels toward himself. Think about it. When things are going well in a man's career, in his investments, or in some of his pursuits, he will tend to feel better about himself. Perhaps he brings home trophies from the marathon he ran on the weekend, or the stocks he trades are on a roll. A successful man is going to have a greater natural tendency to treat his wife with greater respect and dignity. The sad fact is that the opposite is also true. If a man drags his weary body home from work every evening feeling like a failure, if he hasn't had a raise in years, if he is driving the same car he did since college, if he looks at himself in the mirror and sees his hairline receding, and if there is no area of life that is affirming his worth—this man will have less to give to his wife. In fact, this man will tend to be potentially abusive.

Fact: A man will feel toward himself the way he treats his wife. A man who finds opportunity to show grace and kindness, patience, forbearance, forgiveness, gentleness, or self-control toward his wife will in turn feel far better toward himself. He will receive back for his own benefit the honor that he initiates toward his wife. On the other hand, when a man fails to generate honor and grace toward his wife, but instead heaps on her judgment, criticism, disgrace, or abuse, he will tragically receive the same barrenness back into his own life. When such a man who does not like himself begins to expose his frustration with himself against his wife, he will receive back double trouble. He is lashing out at the only one who can potentially lift him up. In a sense, we as men choose the environment that will characterize our home. We set the tone. To put it positively, the better a man feels about himself, the better he treats his wife. And, the better he treats his wife, the better he feels toward himself.

This brilliant insight did not originate with me: It comes right from the Bible. "In this same way, husbands ought to love their wives as their own bodies. He who loves his wife loves himself. After all, no one ever hated his own body, but he feeds and cares for it" (Ephesians 5:28–29).

A man has the opportunity to deliberately treat his wife with honor and respect. If he does, he will in turn receive back double honor. Not only will his wife benefit from the care and affection he shows to her, but being married to such a special lady will enable him at the same time to feel better about himself. "You can't feel like lunch meat if you're served on fine china!"

Rare Air

Removing the Limburger smell of a bad attitude from a marriage requires more than a pep talk. When a man realizes the problem is right under his own nose, he still needs some air freshener.

This poem is the most commonly read lyric at weddings—and for good reason. It speaks of rare air:

> Love is patient,
>   love is kind.
> It does not envy,
>   it does not boast,
>   it is not proud.
> It is not rude,
>   it is not self-seeking,
>   it is not easily angered,
>   it keeps no record of wrongs.
> Love does not delight in evil,
>   but rejoices with the truth.
> It always protects,
>   always trusts
>   always hopes
>   always perseveres.
> Love never fails.
>   —1 Corinthians 13:4–8

This rare air of love is available to every man in his marriage. Such love is the direct result of the presence of Jesus in a relationship. In fact, you can reread the verses and easily substitute *Jesus* for the word *love*.

The portrait of love painted here is humanly impossible. We could never consistently generate this high octane love on our own. But what is not independently possible to us is fully possible when Jesus has His way in us and through us. When a man chooses to love his wife the way Jesus loves us, he is able to enjoy the clean, fresh atmosphere of God's own Spirit. Our home actually becomes His home, and the benefits of His presence are evident. One of the most common indications that we have regained contact with this kind of love is that your marriage will experience a renaissance.

We are all too familiar with the *but-we-don't-love-each-other-anymore* line, or the *I-used-to-feel-love-for-her-but-now-my-love-is-dead* line. Unfortunately, we have accepted the idea that love is somehow temporary, elusive, disposable, faddish, or at least circumstantial. We have convinced ourselves that under "marriage struggles," we need some new romantic feeling, an infatuation, an impulse, a hot sensual attraction. Perhaps we've watched too many Hollywood movies or read too many cheap romance novels, because all such thoughts about love are shallow and grossly inadequate.

To the contrary, love is not a feeling; it is a choice. It is not temporary; it is eternal. Marriage is not disposable or faddish; it is lifelong and indelible. The vow taken on our wedding day sticks like super glue—we do not separate without seriously damaging both ourself and our wife.

If you have read this far and the thought of sticking with the same woman for a lifetime still sounds like life imprisonment—it doesn't need to. You do not need a new wife. You simply need to open the windows and get some fresh spiritual air.

Bottom line: You don't need marriage counseling, or a marriage clinic, or a marriage seminar. What you and I need is Jesus and a fresh infusion of His transforming love. His love is not mystical or intangible; it is practical, relevant, and revitalizing. When the fresh air of God's presence is at work in our heart and our home, I don't need to accept the *my-love-is-dead* or *but-we-don't-love-each-other-anymore* stuff. His love always protects, always trusts, always hopes, always perseveres. His love never fails. If we ever loved our spouse, we don't need to fear our love growing stale. All we need to do is open our windows and receive refreshment from God's own Spirit.

———————

Sometimes I sincerely wonder how many married men ever discover what true love is all about. We see so few examples. Put on your hiking boots. We are about to scale the marital heights with a man who knows how to keep that promise.

Even When It Hurts

Marriage is not built on a single choice the day of the wedding, but on a series of hard choices made throughout a lifetime. Hard choices are what marriages are made of.

The Hebrew songwriter asked his God, "Lord, who may dwell in your sanctuary? Who may live on your holy hill?" A significant part of his answer was this: "He . . . who keeps his oath even when it hurts" (see Psalm 15). I want to introduce you to a man who qualifies.

Early in their marriage, Dr. Robertson McQuilkin and his wife learned Japanese and invested twelve years serving as career missionaries half a world away. They were then asked to move to Columbia, South Carolina, and assume the presidency of the Bible College and Theological Seminary of which his father was the first president. After twenty-two dynamic, fruitful years of devoted leadership, for the first time in his life, Dr. McQuilkin found himself torn between his two life commitments—as president of Columbia Bible College and Theological Seminary and as husband to his wife, who had just been diagnosed with Alzheimer's disease. The editors of *Christianity Today* first asked Dr. McQuilkin to share his story. We reprint it here with his permission.

Just sit back and without interruption listen to him describe his devotion to his wife. It resonates with dignity. It might not be a bad idea to read it with your handkerchief handy.

It has been a decade since that day, during a Florida vacation, when Muriel, my wife, repeated to the couple we were visiting the story she had told just five minutes earlier. *Funny,* I thought, *that's never happened before.* But it began to happen occasionally.

Three years later, when Muriel was hospitalized for tests on her heart, a young doctor called me aside. "You may need to think about the possibility of Alzheimer's," he said. I was incredulous. *These young doctors are so presumptuous and insensitive.* Muriel was doing the same things she had always done, for the most part. True, we had stopped entertaining in our home—no small loss for the president of a thriving seminary and Bible college. She was a great cook and hostess, but she was having increasing difficulty planning menus. Family meals she could handle, but with guests we could not risk missing a salad and dessert, for example.

And, yes, she was having uncommon difficulty painting a portrait of me, which the college and seminary board—impressed by her earlier splendid portrait of my predecessor—had requested. But Alzheimer's? While I had barely heard of the disease, a dread began to lurk around the fringes of my consciousness.

When her memory deteriorated further, we went to Joe Tabor, a neurologist friend, who gave her the full battery of tests and, by elimination, confirmed that she had Alzheimer's. But because she had none of the typical physical deterioration, there was some question. We went to the Duke University Medical Center, believing we should get the best available second opinion. My heart sank as the doctor asked her to name the Gospels and she looked pleadingly at me for help. But she quickly bounced back and laughed at herself. She was a little nervous, perhaps, but nothing was going to get her down.

This time I accepted the verdict. And I determined from the outset not to chase around the country after every new "miracle" treatment we might hear about. Little did I know the day was coming when we would be urged—on average, once a week—to pursue every variety of treatment: vitamins, exorcism, chemicals, this guru, that healer, the other clinic. How could I even look into them all, let alone pursue them? I was grateful to friends who made suggestions, because each was an expression of love. But for us, we would trust the Lord to work a miracle in Muriel if He so desired, or work a miracle in me if He did not.

One day the WMHK station manager, the program manager, and the producer of my wife's morning radio program *Looking Up* asked for an appointment. I knew an occasional program she had produced was not used, but the response to her monologue of upbeat encouragement continued to be strong. Though the program was designed for women, businessmen often told me how they arranged their morning affairs so they could catch the program.

As the appointment began, the three executives seemed uneasy. After a few false starts, I caught on. They were reluctantly letting me know that an era was ending. Only months before, they had talked of national syndication. I tried to help them out. "Are you meeting with me to tell us that Muriel cannot continue?" They seemed relieved that their painful message was out and none of them had to say it. *So,* I thought, *her public ministry is over.* No more conferences, TV, radio. I should have guessed the time had come.

She did not think so, however. She may have lost the radio program, but she insisted on accepting invitations to speak, even though invariably she would come home crushed and bewildered that her train of thought was lost and things did not go well. Gradually, reluctantly, she gave up public ministry.

Still, she could counsel the many young people who sought her out, she could still drive and shop, or write her children. The letters did not always make sense, but then, the children would say, "Mom always was a bit spacy." She also volunteered to read textbooks for a blind graduate student. The plan was to put them on tape so that others could use them. I was puzzled that those responsible never used them, until it dawned on me that reading and writing were going the way of art and public speaking. She was disappointed with each failure and frustration, but only momentarily. She would bounce back with laughter and have another go at it.

Muriel never knew what was happening to her, though occasionally when there was a reference to Alzheimer's on TV she would muse aloud, "I wonder if I'll ever have that?" It did not seem painful for her, but it was a slow dying for me to watch the vibrant, creative, articulate person I knew and loved gradually dimming out.

I approached the college board of trustees with the need to begin the search for my successor. I told them that when the day came that Muriel needed me full time, she would have me. I hoped that would not be necessary till I reached retirement, but at fifty-seven it seemed unlikely I could hold on till sixty-five. They should begin to make plans. But they intended for me to stay on forever, I guess, and made no move. *That's not realistic, and probably not very responsible,* I thought, though I appreciated the affirmation.

So began years of struggle with the question of what should be sacrificed: ministry or caring for Muriel. Should I put the kingdom of God first, "hate" my wife and, for the sake of Christ and the kingdom, arrange for institutionalization? Trusted, life-long friends—wise and godly—urged me to do this.

"Muriel would become accustomed to the new environment quickly." Would she? Would anyone love her at all, let alone love her as I do? I had often seen the empty, listless faces of those lined up in wheelchairs along the corridors of such places, waiting, waiting for the fleeting visit of some loved one. In such an environment, Muriel would be tamed only with drugs or bodily restraints, of that I was confident.

People who do not know me well have said, "Well, you always said, 'God first, family second, ministry third.' " But I never said that. To put God first means that all other responsibilities He gives are first, too. Sorting out responsibilities that seem to conflict, however, is tricky business.

In 1988 we planned our first family reunion since the six children had left home, a week in a mountain retreat. Muriel delighted in her children and grandchildren, and they in her. Banqueting with all those gourmet cooks, making a quilt that pictured our life, scene by scene, playing games, singing, picking wild mountain blueberries was marvelous. We planned it as the celebration of our "fortieth" anniversary, although it was actually the thirty-ninth. We feared that by the fortieth she would no longer know us.

But she still knows us—three years later. She cannot comprehend much, nor express many thoughts, and those not for sure. But she knows whom she loves, and lives in happy oblivion to almost everything else.

She is such a delight to me. I don't *have* to care for her, I *get* to. One blessing is the way she is teaching me so much—about love, for example, God's love. She picks flowers outside—anyone's—and fills the house with them.

Lately she has begun to pick them inside, too. A friend had given us a beautiful Easter lily, two stems with four or five lilies on each, and more to come. One day I came into the kitchen and there on the windowsill over the sink was a vase with a stem of lilies in it. I've learned to "go with the flow" and not correct irrational behavior. She means no harm and does not understand what should be done, nor would she remember a rebuke. Nevertheless, *I* did the irrational—I told her how disappointed I was, how the lilies would soon die, the buds would never bloom, and please do not break off the other stem.

The next day our youngest son, soon to leave for India, came from Houston for his next-to-last visit. I told Kent of my rebuke of his mother and how bad I felt about it. As we sat on the porch swing, savoring each moment together, his mother came to the door with a gift of love for me: she carefully laid the other stem of lilies on the table with a gentle smile and turned back into the house. I said simply, "Thank you." Kent said, "You're doing better, Dad!"

Muriel cannot speak in sentences now, only in phrases and words, and often words that make little sense: "no" when she means "yes," for example. But she can say one sentence, and she says it often: "I love you."

She not only says it, she acts it. The board arranged for a companion to stay in our home so I could go to the office daily. During those two years it became increasingly difficult to keep Muriel home. As soon as I left, she would take out after me. With me she was content; without me, she was distressed, sometimes terror stricken. The walk to school is a mile round trip. She would make that trip as many as ten times a day. Sometimes at night, when I helped her undress, I found bloody feet. When I told our family doctor, he choked up. "Such love," he said simply. Then after a moment, "I have a theory that the characteristics developed across the years come out at times like these." I wish I loved God like that—desperate to be near Him at all times. Thus she teaches me, day by day.

Friends and family often ask, "How are you doing?" meaning, I would take it, "How do you feel?" I am at a loss to respond. There is that subterranean grief that will not go away. I feel just as alone as if I had never known her as she was, I suppose, but the loneliness of the night hours comes because I did know her. Do I grieve her loss or mine? Further, there is the sorrow that comes from my increasing difficulty in meeting her needs.

But I guess my friends are asking not about her needs but about mine. Or perhaps they wonder, in the contemporary jargon, how I am "coping," as they reflect on how the reputed indispensable characteristics of a good marriage have slipped away, one by one.

I came across the common contemporary wisdom in this morning's newspaper in a letter to a national columnist: "I ended the relationship because it wasn't meeting my needs," the writer explained. The counselor's response was predictable: "What were your needs that didn't get met by him in the relationship? Do you still have these same needs? What would he have to do to fill these needs? Could he do it?" Needs for communication, understanding, affirmation, common interests, sexual fulfillment—the list goes on. If the needs are not met, split. He offered no alternatives.

I once reflected on the eerie irrelevance of every one of those criteria for me. But I am not wired for introspection; I am more oriented outward and toward action and the future. I even feel an occasional surge of exhilaration as I find my present assignment more challenging than running an institution's complex ministry. Certainly greater creativity and flexibility are needed.

I have long lists of "coping strategies," which have to be changed weekly, sometimes daily. Grocery shopping together may have been recreation, but it is not so much fun when Muriel begins to load other people's carts and take off with them, disappearing into the labyrinth of supermarkets aisles. Or how do you get a person to eat or take a bath when she steadfastly refuses? It is not like meeting a $10 million budget or designing a program to grasp some emerging global opportunity, to be sure. And it is not as public or exhilarating. But it demands greater resources than I could have imagined, and thus highlights more clearly than ever my own inadequacies, as well as provides constant opportunity to draw on our Lord's vast reservoir of resources.

As she needed more and more of me, I wrestled daily with the question of who gets me full time—Muriel or Columbia Bible College and Seminary? Dr. Tabor advised me not to make the decision based on my desire to see Muriel stay contented. "Make your plans apart from that question. Whether or not you can be successful in your dreams for the college and seminary or not, I cannot judge, but I can tell you now, you will not be successful with Muriel."

When the time came, the decision was firm. It took no great calculation. It was a matter of integrity. Had I not promised, forty-two years before, "in sickness and in health . . . till death do us part"?

This was no grim duty to which I was stoically resigned, however. It was only fair. She had, after all, cared for me for almost four decades with marvelous devotion; now it was my turn. And such a partner she was! If I took care of her for forty years, I would never be out of her debt.

But how could I walk away from the responsibility of a ministry God had blessed so remarkably during our twenty-two years at Columbia Bible College and Seminary?

Not easily. True, many dreams had been fulfilled. But so many dreams were yet on the drawing board. And the peerless team God had brought together—a team not just of top professionals, but of dear friends—how could I bear to leave them? Resignation was painful; but the right path was not difficult to discern. Whatever Columbia needed, it did not need a part-time, distracted leader. It is better to move out and let God designate a leader to step in while the momentum surges.

No, it was not a choice between two loves. Sometimes that kind of choice becomes necessary, but this time responsibilities did not conflict. I suppose responsibilities in the will of God never conflict (though my evaluation of those responsibilities is fallible). Am I making the right choice at the right time in the right way? I hope so. This time it seemed clearly in the best interest of the ministry for me to step down, even if the board and administrators thought otherwise. Both loves—for Muriel and for Columbia Bible College and Seminary—dictated the same choice. There was no conflict of loves, then, or of obligations.

I have been startled by the response to the announcement of my resignation. Husbands and wives renew marriage vows, pastors tell the story to their congregations. It was a mystery to me until a distinguished oncologist who lives constantly with dying people told me, "Almost all women stand by their men; very few men stand by their women." Perhaps people sensed this contemporary tragedy and somehow were helped by a simple choice I considered the only option.

It is all more than keeping promises and being fair, however. As I watch her brave descent into oblivion, Muriel is the joy of my life. Daily I discern new manifestations of the kind of person she is, the wife I always loved. I also see fresh manifestations of God's love—the God I long to love more fully.

Robertson McQuilkin resigned as president of Columbia Bible College and Seminary in 1990. What a man!

Dr. McQuilkin, I for one honor you for making the right choice. Thanks for teaching us all what it really means to keep that promise. You are living in dignity.

Reattached

Sometimes it goes like this: No matter how much we know, and no matter how hard we try, it seems impossible to express love to our wife in terms she can understand. We try to reach out and make contact, but we just don't connect. It's almost as if our arms have been ripped off.

John Wayne Thompson left the house late Saturday morning to do some farm chores. His parents were out of town for the weekend, but 250 squealing pigs were waiting for their barley breakfast. This was one chore John had performed a thousand times on his family's North Dakota farm. Only this time something went haywire.

The January air was crisp. He backed the dump truck to the auger, connected the power takeoff to a shaft on the tractor. He opened the end gate to the truck to dump the grain, started the tractor, and walked back to watch the swine chow down. He hadn't noticed the ice patch behind the truck. He slipped. His shirt tail got caught in the auger shaft. He was instantly yanked to the ground and spun around the shaft half a dozen times.

"I couldn't feel my left arm. I couldn't see my right arm. I thought it was bent back, but when I went to pick myself up, my arms were gone. I started screaming for about five seconds, but then I realized I had to get back to the house before I bled to death."

Somehow he managed to walk up the 300-foot icy slope to his house.

"I had a bone sticking out of my left arm and I thought I could use it to open the lock, but that didn't work. . . . But then there is another door with a round doorknob. I don't know how, but I opened it with my mouth."

He dialed the phone with a pen tip. Seven digits. No one home. He tried again.

Finally . . . "Hello."

"Tammy, you've got to get an ambulance."

"What's the matter?"

"I can't feel my arms. They're gone."

"Who is this?"

"It's John."

The phone went dead.

When she arrived John was in the bathtub, weeping. He didn't want Tammy to see him without any arms. Not wanting to get any blood on the carpet, he stayed in the bathtub for twenty minutes or so until the ambulance arrived.

They gave him oxygen. They wrapped him in sheets and blankets. He had lost nearly half his blood, and by the time he arrived at the hospital his body had jolted into what is known as "compensation shock"—the blood vessels constrict to preserve sufficient blood for the vital organs. The emergency room prepared for double upper-arm reattachment, a surgery previously performed only ten times in the United States.

John's eighteen-year-old body was in excellent shape. The anticipated twelve-hour surgery was complete in half the time. *USA Today* called it "incredible." The New York *Times* called it "incredible." ABC's *Good Morning America,* "a miraculous tale." As the news spread, letters began pouring in from all over the country. Thousands of letters every day. Phone calls from celebrities, including the President. The operation was a complete success. Three weeks later when he left the hospital, he motioned to the cheering crowd with a partially upraised arm.

"People say I'm brave, but inside I'm a chicken." He told reporters, "I hate being called a hero because I didn't do anything for anybody else. I'm glad it's helping other people, but I don't think I'm a hero for saving my own life. I'm just a North Dakota kid, I guess. I'm tough and I don't give up."

John may not be a hero. But he is a good man. A model for the rest of us.

Detached

Millions of men feel as if their arms have been ripped off. Physically, they may not have lost a single appendage, but deep inside they are torn to pieces over the fact that there is a communication gap between themselves and their wives.

A man gets tired of trying to sustain a marriage that is increasingly one-sided. We think, *How long can I give and give without getting anything in return? I feel as if I'm working myself to death to sustain my family's lifestyle, and all I get for it is grief.* A man said to me last week, "I've spent my whole adult life with the same woman, yet after all these years she still feels like a stranger." There is nothing worse than feeling lonely within our own home.

It hurts. It stinks. We get the shaft. But how do we respond? Just lie on the ground and bleed? Scream, with no one to hear? There is no dignity in that.

As men, we want to get reattached to our lives. We want to learn to reach out. To risk. To embrace. To touch and be touched again. But where do we start? It's confusing.

Relationships are not always predictable. They cannot be pre-programmed. Just when we think we have figured out our wives, we hit a slippery spot we had not noticed; and suddenly we are flat on our backs or spinning in circles, not knowing which way is up. When we come to our senses it seems as though we've lost contact with our wives. The most important relationship—which has already absorbed more time, effort, energy and MasterCard receipts than we ever anticipated—is now back at square one. Our marriage is in trouble and we scramble to open doors, dial numbers, find some answers. Even 911 is busy. We experience psychological shock. All other relationships momentarily shut down out of self-preservation. Deep down our souls are crying out for only one thing—plain and simple—we want to be reattached, to feel the power of our arms again. We want to be able to hug the one person with whom we are closest and we want to be able to feel them hug us in return. *Is that asking for too much?* There is nothing worse than having someone in our life we want to squeeze and yet not having any arms. Nothing is more painful. Nothing. Unless, perhaps, it is having the arms to reach out and yet having no one to receive the embrace. No one who cares.

Reattaching our arms so that we can wholeheartedly embrace our wives is what this book is all about. Our goal is not to enable us to become national heroes. We do not expect to receive phone calls from the President, nor will we collect thousands of pieces of fan mail. We just want to be men who do a pretty good job expressing love and kindness in terms our wives can understand.

The critical issue of husbanding is how to become reattached. Foremost Christian psychologist Dr. James Dobson has stated, "If America is going to survive, it will be because husbands and fathers begin to put their families at the highest level of priorities and reserve something of their time, effort, and energy for leadership within their own homes."

Tragically, many men have become detached. As Andrew Chrerlin of Johns Hopkins University said, "Today's children are the first generation in this country's history who think divorce and separation are a normal part of family life."* From 1950 to 1980, the annual rate of illegitimate births increased by a staggering 450%. More than 700,000 children are born every year into homes without fathers, which accounts for almost 19.4% of all children born. More and more sociology reports come to the same conclusion: The common denominator among youth who are involved in serious crime is a missing father.

My own experience of eighteen years of pastoral ministry and youth ministry supports these statistics. The all-too-familiar complaint I hear from married women is, "My husband doesn't have a clue how to express love to me or the kids." Hopefully by now we have more than a clue how to reconnect. Emotionally, spiritually, it is time to come home.

U.S. News and World Report (August 9, 1982), p. 58.

Home

When it comes right down to it, it's impossible to run away from home. No matter how hard we may try, we can't get away from it. It goes with us wherever we go. We can pack our bags, leave our wives, kids, and current address—we can travel across the country; we can start a new relationship with some hot "squeeze." But no matter how hard we try we cannot leave home. It has the incredible ability to catch up to us.

Home is far more than where we hang our jockey shorts. Home reflects our personality, our values, our priorities, our ambitions, our aspirations. Home doesn't start at 6:15 in the evening, when our car pulls into the driveway. Home is twenty-four hours. It doesn't matter whether it is a tenement in the lower east side, or a 6,000-square-foot estate in the country. The size of our acreage or the size of our mortgage has nothing to do with it. Home is a reflection on the outside of who we are on the inside. *Home is who we are.*

Dignity comes to a man who keeps his heart at home. To a man who quits running away from his responsibilities. To a man who dares to live by the promise he has made. To a man who develops virtuous character by walking long in the same direction. To a man who walks humbly before his God.

It is an impossibility, no matter how hard he may try, for a man to find dignity by running away from home, because running away from home means he is running away from himself. Without a home a man lacks a heart. He lacks a root system. He lacks character. He lacks everything that makes a man a man.

When a man decides to come home he decides to grow up. He decides it's time to put the folly of childhood away and begin moving into maturity. Coming home is when a man says, *Yes, I assume responsibility for my own actions. You can hold me accountable. You can look for me, I'll be there.*

When a man decides to come home, there is a sigh of relief that can be heard around the community.

- It is the sigh of a wife who longs to be cherished.
- The sigh of a child who has been inwardly reaching for a daddy.

- The sigh of a generation that has been crumbling for lack of real men.
- The sigh of the man himself who can now loosen his tie, kick off his shoes, and know he is home to stay.

Squeeze

As men we have an inbred desire to find an object for our affection. There is a sense in which this desire is so instinctive, it is an evidence of being created in God's image. Just as God desires intimacy with us, so we desire intimacy with each other. Even ancient Hebrew literature records, "And God saw it was not good for man to be alone" (Genesis 2:18). Because this desire for life-time companionship is such a part of who we are, the level to which we successfully fulfill the desire is the extent to which we will be fulfilled.

A friend told me last week, "Fred, I feel like I should know all the answers. I've read the best marriage books, I've been to marriage enrichment seminars, I've taught the young married couples' Sunday school class—I've even counseled other couples having marriage problems. But meanwhile I lost it. I feel nothing for my wife. Last night she told me our marriage is dead. When she told me those words I felt nothing. Even though she never said them before, they sounded like old news. I don't know what happened, but for some reason all the answers I have heard over the years are doing me no good."

Sometimes we don't need answers—we need arms. We need passion and compassion that reaches out and draws our wives back to our side where they belong. Perhaps it's more than coincidence that the Bible indicates when God made a wife for Adam, He took her from the man's side. Ever since then, it has been man's joy and responsibility to draw his wife back to that original spot.

We call this inner desire in a man to find a single object of his affection *the desire to squeeze*. Don't misunderstand. This desire to squeeze is not simply physical or sexual. Our masculinity is not determined according to the size of our biceps. Instead, our masculinity is determined in part by how effectively we can embrace our wife and draw her close to our side. A squeeze that pleases only ourselves is no squeeze at all. It needs to transmit a level of pleasure to our wife.

To set the record straight, the squeezes I mean are not all physical.

- Catching each other's eye across a crowded room.
- A phone call in the middle of the day.
- A love note.
- Flowers, even when they are picked by the side of the road.
- A walk around the block.
- A back rub.
- Fulfilling a domestic duty—like washing her whitewalls.
- An "I-forgive-you."
- A "can-we-pray-together?"
- An "it's okay—we-can-wait-till-tomorrow-night."
- A heart question.
- A "will-you-forgive-me?"
- An "I love you"—with no strings attached.

In order for a gesture to qualify as a legitimate squeeze, it must connect on both sides: It needs to mean love on the part of the husband, and it must be received as love on the part of the wife. Discovering which expressions connect is what I mean by becoming *reattached*.

This is the kind of love that healthy marriages are made of. It is healthy for the wives. They will thrive on it. But it is also healthy for us as men.

A Living Legacy

No matter how hard a man works, no matter how much wealth and notoriety a man accumulates, no matter how many frequent flier miles he logs, it is always a fair question to ask, *What will I leave behind?*

What we leave behind is called *legacy*. It's more than bank accounts, IRAs and real estate. It is more than "Salesman of the Year" plaques. More than newspaper clippings. And certainly more than a wooden box planted six feet deep in the earth when it is all over. More than a fleeting memory, a legacy is an indelible impression. It is the mark we make in life that lives far longer than forty, fifty, or eighty years. It's the footprints we leave at a workplace or institution, and the fingerprints we leave in the lives we love. It's the way we do things and the reason we do them. Legacy is as close as we can get to immortality this side of eternity.

Deep in the soul of every man is the desire to leave behind a good name. A name that rings true. A name that makes people nod in affirmation. Few men lust for a name that makes people stand up and clap. For most of us a pat on the back from a family member is fine. If we hear a word of encouragement, it may be enough to get our heart out of rhythm. For a man to be able to look into the eyes of his wife and children and to be able to see them looking back with respect, admiration, trust, loyalty—that is enough to make most of us hallucinate. That is a living legacy. And that is what every man longs for.

A living legacy doesn't grow in a vacuum. Neither does it grow in a petri dish. A living legacy is the product of the consistent hard choices we have been talking about—integrity, sensitivity, humility, responsibility, fidelity, and charity. There are no shortcuts. No such thing as microwave maturity. A good name doesn't grow on trees and it is not for sale at any price. It is not just given to an elite few, nor is it withheld from others. It is held out to each of us—ours for the taking—as long as we are willing to pay the price.

Back to Normal

Less than four months after John Thompson's arms were reattached, he graduated from Bowden High School. He admitted it felt good to receive his diploma, but he looked forward to getting back to what he called "normal life." He was tired of all the interviews, all the press conferences, all the phone calls. He anticipates regaining the use of his hands so he can help his dad with the crops. "I'd like to tell them all to leave me alone. . . . I just want to try to get back to normal."

Doing well in the normal stuff of life is what makes a marriage work. It's not the trips to Honolulu. It's not the diamond necklaces or the new Lexus. Where a man earns his dignity is in the common, everyday activities like changing the light bulb and balancing the checkbook.

And what is it that keeps a man faithful to his wife?

Somewhere down under a man's skin . . . down deep where the juices of life flow . . . down where a man's soul is as big as the Grand Canyon . . . down where he knows right from wrong . . . down where he decides how he wants to be remembered and what he wants to be remembered for . . . down where a man is capable of catching a glimpse of God before whom he will one day stand and give an account—it is down there where a man makes the hard choices necessary to build a life of dignity for his wife, his family, his God, and for himself. At that bedrock level, the absence of dignity will crush a man's spirit, but the presence of dignity will give him the confidence that he has not lived in vain.

Fact: None of us knew what we were doing when we got married. There we stood, dressed in our little tuxedos, waiting innocently for our wives to be escorted down the aisle. On the outside we were smiling from ear to ear like punching dummies, and inside we were scared spitless. When it came to marriage, we didn't have a clue. Ignoramuses. We might have thought someone could have warned us about a few of the challenges we'd face. No way. Like cattle, we were full-grown men being led to slaughter.

Now, here we are years later, feeling as if we've been stuck in a time warp. Dates have changed, kids have been born, our hair is receding, our wives are not looking any younger and yet we don't have much to show for it.

Stop. . . .

Let me set the record straight. If we feel that our marital report card is somewhere in the *B-* and *C+* range, we may actually be better off than when we entered marriage feeling as though we would *ace* the course without even attending classes. When we reach a true estimation of ourselves, we are well on our way to becoming men of dignity.

If as a man and husband, you have felt home alone, unable to get the front door open, feeling as though your arms have been ripped off, unable to dial the phone, unable to get an answer, unable to make contact, there is hope, there is help, and there is dignity. Despite the fact that every nerve ending in your body may be screaming its head off, you can be reattached. You can once again reach out and make contact with the one you love.

Maybe you can hear your wife calling, "Honey, are you home?"

Answer her with dignity. "Yes, honey, I'm home. I'm home to stay."

Study Guide Questions

Section 1—There Is Hope

Chapter 1: "Honey, Are You Home?"

1. Respond to the billboard, "More men run away from home than teenagers."
2. What factors can potentially make men feel like packing their bags and leaving home?
3. Why do men at times feel as if they have lost their freedom?
4. In what areas of life do you find dignity? What makes you feel that your life is worth living?
5. What areas of life potentially drain us of dignity?
6. Name a few specific "treadmills."
7. Respond to the statement, "Duty without dignity is deadly."

Chapter 2: The Morning After

1. As the author described his "morning after," can you identify? When did the weight of responsibility in marriage first hit you?
2. What do we mean by the term "married bachelor"? List some qualities that describe him.
3. Have you ever felt like a failure as a husband? In what specific areas of your marriage?

184 / Men and Marriage

4. In what ways can you identify with Ralph?
5. If you were to ask your wife, "Honey, in what ways can I improve as a husband," what might she say?

Chapter 3: Nerds Make Pretty Good Husbands

1. What exactly is the "myth of the natural-born husband"?
2. "We were not born with the skills it requires to excel as men in marriage"—agree or disagree?
3. Why is it hard for men to admit their weaknesses and insecurities to their wives?
4. Respond to the statement, "Nerds make pretty good husbands."
5. Can you identify with Howard? In what specific ways?
6. Who has it harder: the husband who struggles at marriage while succeeding in his career, or the husband who struggles while failing at his career?
7. Do wives expect perfection?
8. Make a list of your expectations of a girl friend before marriage and a separate list of your expectations of your wife after marriage?

Chapter 4: Our Secret Enemy

1. Compare and contrast "twisted pride" with "true dignity."
2. What lesson is illustrated by the ski boat?
3. Can you identify with the ski boat story? What area of your marriage is similiar?
4. Discuss the C. S. Lewis quote.
5. What positive result can we gain when our twisted pride collides with our wife's pride?
6. What strengths can you recognize in your wife? Which of these are greater than your own strengths? How have you responded to these areas?

Chapter 5: How to Win Your Wife's Affection

1. How do you respond to the idea of "winning your wife's affection"?
2. How did Peter respond to the idea?
3. If you had counseled Peter, what would you have said?

4. What is the point of "Easter chicks" illustration? Have you ever observed a man compulsive in his marriage who virtualy "loved her to death" by smothering her? Describe it.
5. Define in your own words the "100% principle."
6. How do you respond to Elizabeth Taylor's "51% principle"?
7. Why does Jesus serve as a positive role model for marriage?
8. Is there a particular line in Don Francisco's song with which you can identify?

Section 2—There Is Help

Chapter 6: "But I Still Can't Figure Her Out"

1. What do we mean by "juice"?
2. Can you identify with Jarvis's frustration in not being able to figure out his wife? What aspect of your wife's personality has been confusing to you at times?
3. Have you ever asked, "Why can't a woman be more like a man?"
4. What lesson do you learn from the coal miner?
5. How do the two skills—being considerate and treating them with respect—relate to each other?
6. Define "heart questions." What do they communicate to a wife?

Chapter 7: "What Do You Do?"

1. Has your wife ever complained about your job?
2. How did her complaints make you feel?
3. Is it fair for our wives to expect us to treat them as being more important than our careers?
4. Why do men often fail to communicate greater importance to their wives?
5. Which of the "five ways to convince your wife" do you see as profitable?
6. What lesson can we learn from the "dump truck" illustration?

Chapter 8: Mutual Sexual Fulfillment

1. Discuss this statement, "Any mammal can reach orgasm. . . . It requires a certain degree of skill to experience consistent mutual sexual fulfillment."

2. Is there a particular phrase in Mike Mason's description you enjoy?
3. Can you identify with Kurt's frustration?
4. Which of the five principles shared with Kurt sound helpful to you?
5. Do you find the suggestions—Purity in the Work Place/Any Place—helpful? Or are they unnecessary?
6. Would it be helpful to consistently meet with a group of men to ask the six accountability questions?

Chapter 9: Better Than Sex

1. What lesson can we learn from "the plague"?
2. What situation in marriage have you faced that is similar to "the plague"?
3. What discovery helped Troy and Brenda's marriage?
4. Thoughtfully answer the question, "Are you friends with your wife?" What evidence do you have to support your answer?
5. What area of your life is still difficult to talk about with your wife? Why?
6. When Sherry interrupted, "Why don't you ever let me meet any of your needs?" what was she asking for?
7. Can you identify an area of personal weakness you could open up to your wife's strength?

Chapter 10: True Intimacy

1. Why do men feel intimidated when it comes to talking about God?
2. How would you respond if you knew your wife wanted to pray with you on a daily basis?
3. Often a man who has a personal relationship with Jesus still avoids praying with his wife. Why?
4. Do you know for certain that when you die you will go to heaven?
5. Suppose you were to die and stand before God and He were to ask you, "Why should I let you into my heaven?" What would you say to Him?
6. What are some advantages of praying together with our spouse?

7. Which of the practical suggestions on praying together do you find most helpful?

Section 3—There Is Dignity

Chapter 11: Faithfulness Under Fire

1. List qualities of true friendship.
2. What aspects of friendship are illustrated by the soldier who died carrying his friend back to the foxhole?
3. What insights helped Kevin make friends with his wife?
4. Has your wife ever made you feel "castrated"?
5. What is mean by "yield the right of way"?
6. What does "yielding the right of way" have to do with friendship in marriage?
7. Essentially, what is the difference between "yielding the right of way" and simply "giving in"?
8. Respond to the statement, "Yielding the right of way says *I love you* in a language wives can understand."

Chapter 12: The Winner's Circle

1. How do you respond to the pro golfer who adjusted his score card? Clap, boo, shake your head in disbelief?
2. The chapter makes several attempts to define dignity. Try to define it in your own words.
3. What do the two words "my bad" have to do with a successful marriage?
4. Physical sexual fidelity is a given. What is meant by "mental fidelity" and why is it equally important?
5. Make your own list of five or six ingredients you think are significant in order for dignity to be present in a marriage.

Chapter 13: Fresh Air

1. What does the story about stuffy air in the office illustrate?
2. What is meant by "fresh air"?
3. Respond to the statement "it's a man's responsibility to make sure his home has plenty of fresh air."
4. Specifically, what factors contribute to "housatosis"?

5. Why is it so important for husbands to provide *order* in the home for the sake of their wives?
6. "A man treats his wife the way he feels toward himself." Respond.

Chapter 14: Even When It Hurts

1. Why was Dr. Robertson McQuilkin's story chosen to illustrate a married man who keeps his promise even when it hurts?
2. "Marriage is not built on a single choice the day of the wedding, but on a series of hard choices made throughout a lifetime." Respond.
3. Using Dr. McQuilkin as a case study, what specific qualities do you find that make him a successful "promise keeper"?
4. "I don't have to care for her, I get to." What does this statement tell us?
5. What tangible benefits are coming back to Dr. McQuilkin for all the love he is showing to his wife?

Chapter 15: Reattached

1. When your wife doesn't understand you, how does it make you feel?
2. Why does the author say, "It is impossible to run away from home"?
3. "Dignity comes to a man who dares to stay at home." Respond.
4. Make your own list of at least a dozen specific, tangible ways that you can say to your wife, "I love you."
5. Write a note to your wife telling her about your choice to treat her with dignity and to leave her a legacy.
6. In your own words, tell her you're home to stay.